# of ONTARIO HISTORY

Intriguing and Entertaining Facts about our Province's Past

René Biberstein

BLUE
BIKE
BOOKS

The Publisher: Blue Bike Books

Library and Archives Canada Cataloguing in Publication

Biberstein, René, 1981–
   Bathroom book of Ontario history / René Josef Biberstein ; Roger Garcia, Roly Woods, illustrators.

(Bathroom books of Canada ; 9)
ISBN-13: 978-1-897278-16-1
ISBN-10: 1-897278-16-0

   1. Ontario—History—Miscellanea. I. Garcia, Roger, 1976–
II. Title. III. Series.

FC3061.B529 2006   971.3   C2006-904130-X

Project Director: Nicholle Carrière
Project Editor: Alison Ward
Cover Image: Roly Woods
Illustrations: Roly Woods, Roger Garcia

We acknowledge the financial support of the Alberta Foundation for the Arts for our publishing program.

PC: P5

DEDICATION

I dedicate this book to the Toronto Public Library system, arguably the best and most extensive in North America. I hope someday they will accept these words in lieu of payment of my vast overdue fines, incurred during the research for this book, and allow me to make use of their top-rate services again.

ACKNOWLEDGEMENTS

Many thanks, once again, to Laurel Christie for her assistance in finding research materials for me and for feeding me with nutritious foods and vitamin pills.

Thanks also to my editor Alison Ward and to Tim Le Riche, who edited *The Bathroom Book of Ontario Trivia*, my previous book with Blue Bike Books. Both of them have done tremendous work in cleaning up my writing, which is never a small task.

A further note here: I credited coffee for helping me get through my last book. This time, it's given me a serious case of heartburn. Therefore, no more thanks to coffee.

CONTENTS

INTRODUCTION

In Ontario, history is a mystery. I say it's also a running joke. I write this introduction in the greasy, soupy humidity and smog of another record-breaking, hot Toronto summer. It's hard to reconcile this picture with the famously temperate summers of Toronto's past. Black and white photos from the 1920s show thousands of people in full-body bathing suits swimming in the still-clean Lake Ontario, by the old Sunnyside Amusement Park's Roman Bathing Pavilion. (The amusement park is long gone, but the pavilion still stands, a bit run down, acting as a change room for a nearby pool.)

Why does the past seem like a scene from a different planet?

The change in climate parallels an overall lack of historical memory in Ontario. Ask anyone about the history of the province, and you'll mostly get blank stares, quizzical looks, or even bug-eyed fear (attributable to high school history exam flashbacks, no doubt). I remember every history teacher I ever had nail-gunning George Santayana's quote: "Those who cannot remember the past are doomed to repeat it" into my head, as a warning to stay awake through lectures, properly source footnotes and so on. (Those who cannot come up with quotes of their own are condemned to repeat this one, I guess.)

Here's the joke: Ontarians have consistently forgotten their past but have rarely repeated anything. In fact, there has been so little repetition, so many 180-degree turns and so many people with their own visions for Ontario, that every era seems like a new dimension, totally separated from the past.

So why read about Ontario's history at all? And why did I write about it? The same reason anyone writes about anything: it's full of great stories, many of them eccentric, weird, lurid, shocking, good for a laugh, good for a head scratch (or a chin rub) or good for repeating. Ontario's history is populated with characters with funny ideas, sometimes larger than life and sometimes just plain odd. As a matter of habit, I've always found myself collecting trivia and anecdotes and reading up on history—just for the fun of it.

And history does indeed sometimes come back to bite you. (In 2006, for instance, Ontarians got a crash course in history through the media, when the Haudenosaunee from the Six Nations Reserve occupied a road and housing development near Hamilton to protest land that had been taken from them in the 1850s.) Mixed in with everything else—as is the case with all history—is a fair dose of tragedy.

I hope you enjoy this book of Ontario history. Pick it up, put it down and open it up in the middle. And if years later you've forgotten what you read, you're invited—but not condemned—to reread it.

Early Days
(Before 1535)

*What can you say about a time
before written language?*

Unfortunately, today, not much.

ONTARIO BEFORE WRITING

In the Beginning, It Was Really, Really Cold

In 11,000 BC, the time of the earliest known human settlement in Ontario, most of the province was covered in ice. Only the south, from Lake Huron down, and a pocket in the northwest, around Kenora and Thunder Bay, was habitable. Before that, the whole province had been locked under glaciers. Much of the shape of today's province was formed by the movement and melting of the ice. And people complain about the cold today!

What is Ontario? A Brief Explanation

Obviously, Ontario didn't exist in 11,000 BC (or at any time before 1867, for that matter). For the sake of convenience, I've used the term "Ontario," meaning the area that now goes by that name. I've also used the terms "Upper Canada" and "Canada West" during the eras that those terms were used.

DID YOU  KNOW?

Between 5000 and 1000 BC, things started taking shape. Archaeologists say that two distinct cultures developed. In the north, the ancestors of today's Cree appeared. Some of their best-known achievements include the use of canoes and snow-shoes to travel. They began using bows and arrows and hunted caribou, fish, bears and smaller animals.

In the south, the ancestors of the Iroquoian peoples began to fashion a number of new tools, as well as fishhooks, beads, bracelets and combs. They also started to work copper—traded from the people in northern Ontario—into weapons and orna-ments. They were known for taming dogs and using them for hunting but also for adopting more plants into their diets.

Now *That's* Big Game!

Little is known about the people who lived in Ontario at the time of the glaciers. They were nomadic, travelling in family groups and sometimes coming together for bigger gatherings. Their dart heads, knives and others tools remain, but their clothing and houses are long gone. They must have been a brave and hardy bunch—in addition to hunting caribou and other modern game, they also stalked and killed woolly mammoths and mastodons.

Trade You My Shell For…

From 1000 BC to the arrival of Europeans in the 16th century, the North American trading networks saw tremendous expansion. Conch shells from the Gulf of Mexico have been found in Ontario, as have other items from the Canadian East Coast and the U.S. Midwest. Ontario copper was a hot commodity elsewhere. Canoes—and feet—were the only means of transport. Shoes were likely popular items, too!

Trading For Magic Beans

The most dramatic result of the trading network was that agriculture expanded northward. Tobacco began to appear in Ontario around 500 BC. Corn—developed in Mexico in 5000 BC—arrived in 500 AD, and sunflowers, used mainly for their oil, in 1300. Beans and squash arrived in 1400. The people of southern Ontario began to build larger settlements and adopted a stationary, agricultural society. Although they still hunted, fished and gathered, farm vegetables came to make up about 80 percent of their diet.

DID YOU  KNOW?

Ever feel the itch to move and start all over again? What if everyone had the same itch? And what if a move was necessary?

Agriculture allowed people in early southern Ontario to build towns. Some of their settlements may have accommodated over 3000 people and were fortified with palisades, turrets and catwalks. These people lived in longhouses, each with up to 100 residents. Because crop rotation wasn't practised, farmers exhausted the local soil nutrients, and therefore, their environment. Every 15 to 35 years, the whole community had to move to a new place. This also gave a chance for new buildings to be put up, replacing those that were rotting and in poor repair.

Complex Politics

Aboriginal people in Ontario are known for their complicated political structures—almost mind-boggling to outsiders. With agriculture came a complex division of responsibilities between men and women. Men tended to be in charge of hunting and held roles as chiefs and war chiefs (who made decisions in times of war). Women did most of the planting and harvesting of crops and were in charge of the clans and town life. Clans were groups that extended across a nation (and continue to extend across aboriginal nations today). Each clan had its own special skills and traditions, and members of the same clan—even if they weren't related—considered each other like family. As clan matrons, women were often tasked with appointing men to the role of chief. Furthermore, in a single community, there were multiple chiefs and multiple clan matrons who each had specific responsibilities and specific relationships to one another.

The result was (or at least was supposed to be) a happy balance of power between different interests. And in fact, most communities and nations made decisions by consensus.

Mounds of Mounds

Starting around the beginning of the first millennium AD, people in both northern and southern Ontario started building burial mounds. They were often circular, as big as 35 metres in diameter and 8 metres high. The only known animal-shaped grave in Canada—though many exist in the United States—is the Serpent Mound at Rice Lake, near Peterborough, built between 128 and 302 AD. It is 60 metres long and shaped like a curving snake. By the time Europeans arrived in Ontario, people had mostly given up this practice. It seems like a lot of work, anyway.

Early Europeans in Ontario?
Persistent rumours survive about early Viking or Celtic settlements in Ontario. Supporters point to primitive rock pictographs that appear to show boats with sails, something unknown to aboriginal peoples. Historians almost unanimously reject these suggestions; however, one of these fanciful explorers—a Welsh prince named Madoc ad Owaiin Gwynedd, said to have discovered North America in 1170—did have some concrete affect on Ontario. The town of Madoc, north of Belleville, is named after him (though it was built in the 1830s, on a former Mohawk townsite).

Before the Census

Must have been nice—no census takers knocking on your door, no forms to fill out. Unfortunately, no one knows how many people lived in Ontario before Europeans arrived. There are no written records, and many people lived nomadically, moving in and out of what would become the province. But Ontario was far from empty. Historians have estimated that between 50,000 and 200,000 people called the future province home.

Conquest After Conquest: Things Get Violent (1535–1790)

These were (as far as we know) the bloodiest years ever in Ontario.

The arrival of the French set off centuries of culture clash, power struggle, disease and war. It caused the total destruction of several aboriginal nations and the razing of many towns. It also saw the fur trade take off as a multinational business and the founding of the first French settlements in Ontario.

Then, to top it all off, the English arrived, defeated the French and set off a new round of colonization and displacement.

EUROPEANS SHOW UP

You Don't Know Jacques

In 1535, the Breton explorer Jakez Karter (better known by the French translation of his name, Jacques Cartier) sailed up the St. Lawrence River to the Iroquois town of Hochelaga (modern-day Montréal). Although he didn't get as far as Ontario, his influence on the province was substantial. The goods that Cartier brought were traded farther inland, and his visit marked the beginning of major European trade in Québec and Ontario.

Problems Begin

Cartier also caused trouble. He planted a giant cross on the shore of the modern-day Gaspé Peninsula and told the locals (who were naturally curious) that it was an insignificant structure. In fact, it meant that he was claiming the land for France and Christianity. His condescending attitude to the people he met along the St. Lawrence, and his engaging in kidnapping—he infamously nabbed the sons of Chief Donacona of Québec City—gave Cartier a bad reputation. This caused the aboriginal people to temporarily block Europeans from coming farther inland than the Saguenay River.

The goods that Cartier brought with him also caused conflict. When Samuel de Champlain retraced Cartier's steps 75 years later, the people whom Cartier had encountered were gone. They had been defeated and dispersed by nations from farther inland, likely envious of their access to European goods.

DID YOU  KNOW?

Cartier may have been the most influential early European on the scene, but he wasn't the first. By 1520, a few European goods had already reached Ontario from Portuguese, Basque and French fishermen who traded with aboriginal peoples on the East Coast.

THE HAUDENOSAUNEE
(SIX NATIONS OR IROQUOIS CONFEDERACY)

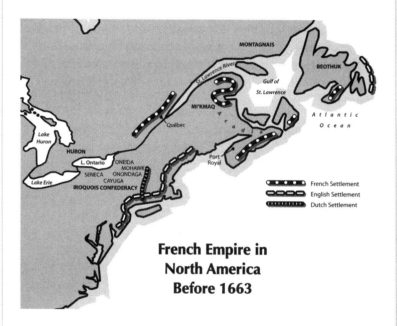

**French Empire in
North America
Before 1663**

The Name Game

The members of the Six Nations, or Iroquois Confederacy, call themselves the Haudenosaunee, or "the people of the longhouse." The word "Haudenosaunee" is coming into more popular use these days, and for the rest of this book I'll call this group of people by that name.

DID YOU  KNOW?

There seems to have been a phenomenon of Europeans naming Native peoples from insults made by their neighbours. (Think of the name "Eskimo" initially given to the Inuit. It was an Algonquian name meaning "eaters of raw flesh.") The European name "Iroquois" is considered to be a French corruption of a derogatory term meaning "black snake," that was given to the Haudenosaunee by their enemies, the Wendat. Today, the name "Iroquoian" is used to describe all of the people—Wendat and Haudenosaunee included—who lived in and around southern Ontario and spoke similar languages.

Six Nations in the House

The homeland of the Haudenosaunee was in upstate New York, around the Finger Lakes. They lived next to one another in their national groups, each group including a number of towns. The Iroquois saw themselves as geographically arranged like a longhouse: the westernmost nation in the confederacy, the Seneca, was called the "keepers of the western door." In the east, the Mohawk were called the "keepers of the eastern door." The Onondaga, in the middle, were called the "keepers of the fire."

The Six Nations of the Confederacy:

Original Name	Meaning	European Name
Onondowahgah	People of the Great Hill	Seneca
Kanien'kéhaka	People of the Flint	Mohawk
Guyohkohnyoh	People of the Great Swamp	Cayuga
Onayotekaono	People of the Upright Stone	Oneida
Onundagaono	People of the Hills	Onondaga
Ska-Ruh-Reh	Shirt-Wearing People	Tuscarora

When Was the Confederacy Formed?

Historians debate the date that the Iroquois Confederacy was established. Modern day Six Nations members say that it originated shortly before the arrival of Europeans, while some archaeologists argue that it was formed shortly afterwards. The date could be between 1400 and 1600.

A Handy Partnership

The legendary co-founders of the Confederacy were Deganawida, known as the Great Peacemaker, and his spokesperson, Hiawatha. Hiawatha was famous as a politician and orator—two things that often went together in the entirely oral culture of the Haudenosaunee. Deganawida was less accomplished in this respect, though he provided most of the content of Hiawatha's speeches. His name means "double tongue," and he is remembered as having a severe speech impediment.

The Other Hiawatha

Hiawatha—or at least his name—is well known to Europeans because of the epic poem, *The Song of Hiawatha*, by the American poet, Henry Wadsworth Longfellow. In fact, the Hiawatha in the poem—who is an Ojibwa living near Lake Superior, a Christian convert and capable of super-human feats—has no relation whatsoever to the real Hiawatha.

Reality Imitates Art

Matters were further confused when the 19-year-old Albert Edward, Prince of Wales visited an Ojibwa community at Rice Lake in 1860. He was inspired by the poem to name the community Hiawatha. The name stuck, though the Ojibwa were the traditional enemies of the Haudenosaunee, to which the real Hiawatha belonged. Today, the village of Hiawatha still exists and its residents call themselves the Ojibwa of Hiawatha First Nation.

Five or Six?

The Confederacy was originally called the Five Nations. In 1720, the Tuscarora Nation, which was forced from its homeland in North Carolina by Europeans, settled between the Oneida and Onondaga. They were accepted as the sixth member of the Confederacy.

Tourism Before Double-Deckers

In 1710, chiefs of four of the five nations were invited to London, England, to meet Queen Anne and be toured around the city. (It is not known what happened to the fifth chief.) The chiefs, incorrectly called "the four Indian kings" by the English media, were exposed to such civilized pastimes as cockfighting and bear baiting. They also took in a performance of *Macbeth* and gave long speeches—an aboriginal specialty—to the royal court. Like all good tourists, the chiefs came back with souvenirs—in this case, a double set of silverware used for church services. It was a gift from Queen Anne, for the new chapel she was building for them in the Mohawk Valley, New York.

One of the chiefs, Tehwaghwengarahkwin, later became the father of Joseph Brant, probably the best-known Haudenosaunee politician of all time. Today (thanks to Brant), most of the souvenir silverware is in the new Mohawk chapel in the Six Nations of the Grand River Reserve near Brantford.

DID YOU KNOW?

The Gayanashagowa, or "Great Law of Peace," laid down the constitution of the Six Nations. Because the Haudenosaunee peoples did not develop written languages until much later, all aspiring politicians had to memorize the constitution.

Federalism...A Haudenosaunee Invention?

There is some evidence that early Americans were impressed by the constitution and structure of the Six Nations. Benjamin Franklin and Thomas Jefferson may have used it as an early inspiration for the federal structure of the United States.

Wampum: Not Money, But Valuable

"Reading" the Gayanashagowa and other laws and agreements, or even stories, was done with the help of wampum, belts of stringed beads that worked as memory aids. Wampum belts could be anywhere between a few decimetres to metres in length. The beads were difficult to make and were usually carved from seashells. Because wampum was valued so highly, Europeans mistakenly thought that it was a form of money— a myth that still exists today.

DID YOU  KNOW?

There is even some evidence of settlers in New England making their own wampum for trade. If they thought it was money, does that make it counterfeiting?

The Hiawatha Belt

One of the most valuable possessions of the Haudenosaunee was the "Hiawatha Belt," a 6574-bead wampum belt dating back to the time of Hiawatha and the Great Law of Peace. It shows four squares with a tree in the middle, all linked together. The objects represent the original Five Nations' geographic positions, with the tree representing the Onondaga. The tree (also sometimes described as a fire or a heart) is also the symbol of the Confederacy. The belt is now in the New York State Museum in Albany.

Six Nations Power

The Haudenosaunee emerged as the big winners of the wars in Ontario and surrounding areas in the 17th century. While other nations and confederacies saw their populations cut in half, or more, by disease, the Haudenosaunee were able to absorb and assimilate enough of their defeated enemies to maintain a stable population. In 1667, they signed a peace treaty with France and were able to control almost all of southern Ontario from their base in New York. To consolidate their hold, they began establishing colonies in Ontario.

Ganatsekwyagon: 17th Century Metropolis

The Seneca built the city of Ganatsekwyagon on a hill overlooking the mouth of the Rouge River, where modern-day Scarborough and Pickering meet. Over 2000 people lived there, making it one of the largest settlements in Canada at the time, though Seneca communities in New York were said to reach populations of 3500. (By contrast, Montréal and Québec City, the biggest European centres in Canada, had about 3000 and 2000 people, respectively.) Later in the 17th century, Ganatsekwyagon divided into several towns known collectively as Gandatsetiagonnes. Teiaiagon, a smaller town, was built at the mouth of the Humber River in the west end of modern Toronto.

Destruction of Ganatsekwyagon

In 1687, the French and Haudenosaunee were at war. The French army, with the help of their new Ojibwa allies, destroyed both towns and killed most of their citizens. In 1689, the Seneca took revenge by attacking Lachine, Québec, and killing nearly 100 people. They went on to besiege Montréal. A new peace treaty was signed in 1701, but by that time, the Ojibwa had begun to permanently settle southern Ontario. The Haudenosaunee did not return to the province in large numbers until after the American Revolution.

THE WENDAT
(HURON CONFEDERACY)

The Confederacy

The archrival of the Six Nations was the Wendat Confederacy. Its homeland, called Huronia today, was in the area between Lake Simcoe and Georgian Bay. The original nations of this confederacy were the Attigneenongnahac and the Attignawantan. The Arendarhonon joined in 1590 and the Tahontaenrat in 1610. A fifth nation, the Ataronchronon, was in a sort of trial membership at the time. The Wendat lived in large farming communities similar to the Iroquois and spoke a related language. They developed friendly relations with the French but were almost completely wiped out by disease and by attacks from the Haudenosaunee.

Huron or Wendat? More Insults
The name Huron comes from a somewhat insulting 16th century French slang word for "a big clump of hair." It could refer to a wild boar, known for the clumps of spiky hair on its head and back or to a peasant whose hair was messy. The Huron were known for their hairstyle, with hair arranged in a spiked row (a style that, ironically, is associated with one of their enemies, the Mohawk). The modern surviving descendants of the Huron call themselves Wendat or Wyandot. The word means "peninsula dweller." In this book, I'll call them the Wendat.

DID YOU KNOW?

The Wendat were known for the massive scale of their cornfields, covering almost 3000 hectares. It was said that, in 17th century Huronia, it was "easier to get lost in a cornfield" than in the forest.

The Rise and Fall of the Wendat

The Wendat became the major trading partner of the French, pushing aside the Algonquian with whom the French had earlier dealt. This position brought them considerable wealth and influence. The prosperity quickly spread throughout the confederacy. As in most aboriginal nations, it was tradition to share goods within the community, and stinginess was considered disrespectful.

In the 1630s, there was a devastating outbreak of smallpox that almost completely wiped out the Wendat. They had traditionally fought with the Haudenosaunee, and things quickly worsened when the Dutch settlers in New York began selling guns to the Mohawk. As the Haudenosaunee started to demand a bigger hunting territory to acquire pelts to trade, they began to attack the Wendat more frequently and destroy their communities. By 1650, the Haudenosaunee completely occupied Huronia.

The attempts by French Jesuits to convert the Wendat to Christianity split the communities between Christians and non-Christians, and the two groups refused to cooperate with one another. From a population of over 30,000 in 1600, less than 1500 Wendat survived in 1650. Those who did either escaped with the French to Québec, or migrated to Ohio and Michigan. Most of these were later forced farther west, to Kansas and Oklahoma.

Take Two Baptisms and Call Me in the Morning

French priests and Wendat in Huronia were notorious for misunderstanding each other's customs. The Wendat initially had trouble interpreting the meanings of conversion and baptism, often thinking of them as cures for sickness. Missionaries were surprised by the sudden vehemence of their converts; when they got sick again, they asked to be re-baptized.

Tricks of the Trade

Priests generally didn't appreciate being thought of as sorcerers by the Wendat, but they weren't above using tricks that the locals considered magic in order to get converts. A popular tactic was to publicly predict eclipses and astronomical changes. These were elements of science that went back to the ancient Greeks, but were considered miraculous by the Wendat.

Sparing the Rod

Jesuit missionaries were shocked to see that Wendat parents refused to beat or punish their children. The missionaries considered that this "lack of discipline" would spoil them. "The Savages love their children above all things," wrote one Jesuit. "They are like the Monkeys—they choke them by embracing them too closely."

The power that Wendat women held also surprised the Jesuits. "A man may promise you something, and if he does not keep his promise, he thinks that he is sufficiently excused when he tells you that his wife did not wish to do it," wrote a missionary. "I told him that he was the master and in France women do not rule their husbands."

DID YOU KNOW?

Every 15 years, Wendat communities held a Feast of the Dead, in which they dug up the remains of everyone who had died since the last feast and buried them in a communal pit. They often invited Europeans and neighbours to come and share in the night of feasting and gift giving.

Rebirth

In 1999, modern-day Wendat from across North America met in Huronia and declared the Huron Confederacy re-established.

THE OTHER IROQUOIANS

The Neutral and Tionnontaté Confederacies

The two other confederacies in southern Ontario, the Neutral and the Tionnontaté, were Iroquoians who spoke similar languages to the Haudenosaunee and Wendat and led a similar farming lifestyle. Tionnontaté (also called the Petun by Europeans) lived just south of the Wendat, on the southern part of Georgian Bay. The Neutral lived in the Niagara, Haldimand and Hamilton areas. They were never actually "neutral," but they got their name from the French, because of their geographic location between the Wendat and the Haudenosaunee and their willingness to trade with both warring nations. Like the Wendat, they were defeated and dispersed by the Haudenosaunee. The Haudenosaunee feared that the Neutral would provide shelter for the Wendat and allow them, with the help of the French, to re-establish themselves. Between 1649 and 1650, the Tionnontaté were overrun, and most of them fled as refugees with the Wendat. In 1651, the Neutral were defeated and dispersed. Some of them were absorbed into the Iroquois, and most fled west to join other nations.

For 50 years afterwards, the Haudenosaunee controlled nearly all of southern Ontario, using it as a giant hunting ground.

I Think I Understand You...
The Wendat and Neutral called each other "Attiwandaronk," which means, "people who speak a slightly different language."

THE ANISHINAABEG AND THE CONFEDERACY OF THREE FIRES

Many Peoples

The Anishinaabeg—a large group of related nations speaking similar dialects, and including the Ottawa, Ojibwa or Chippewa, Potawatomi, Algonquin, Nipissing and Mississauga—came to Ontario from the East Coast sometime before the arrival of Europeans. They settled across the centre of the province, north of the Wendat, from Ottawa to Manitoulin Island, around the north side of Lake Huron and Lake Superior and south on the St. Clair River.

DID YOU  KNOW?

The Algonquin Nation, near the Ottawa River, was the first in Ontario with which the French began to exchange goods. At first, the Algonquin monopolized trade with the French, until France realized that the more numerous Wendat could provide them with more furs.

In 1615, Samuel de Champlain, founder of Québec, ran into Ottawa people for the first time and began trading with them. An alliance formed between the Anishinaabeg and the French and Wendat. French missionaries reported in 1640 that the Ottawa lived mostly on hunting and gathering, but also did some farming, to the extent that the short northern growing season would let them. After the defeat of the Wendat, the Ottawa were forced west, but some later returned to Manitoulin.

Conquest of Southern Ontario

In the second half of the 17th century, the Ojibwa almost completely pushed the Haudenosaunee out of southern Ontario. They set up permanent settlements along the north shore of Lake Ontario, where they began growing crops more intensively and trading with the French. The Ojibwa who moved down to Lake Ontario became known as the Mississauga. The present city of Mississauga, which has a large Ojibwa settlement on the Credit River, is named after them.

The Confederacy of Three Fires

The Anishinaabeg Nations had a difficult relationship with the Haudenosaunee. The Ottawa, Ojibwa and Potawatomi formed the Confederacy of Three Fires to counter the power of the Six Nations Confederacy. They kept their alliance with the French and fought against the British during the War of the Conquest in the 1760s.

Pontiac's War

After the defeat of the French and the British seizure of Ontario, the Anishinaabeg Nations switched their alliance over to the British. The relationship between them soured; however, and the Ottawa war chief Obwandiyag (better known as Pontiac), led a massive rebellion aimed at pushing the British out of the Great Lakes. He failed to capture Fort Detroit, after besieging it for six months, and was forced to sign a peace treaty with the British in 1763.

The war between the British and the Anishinaabeg was the first time biological warfare was deliberately used in North America. British soldiers—pretending to make a peace offering—gave smallpox-infected blankets to the Ojibwa.

The Trojan Lacrosse Ball

During the Pontiac rebellion, the Ottawa captured Fort
Michilmackinac (now in Michigan) from the British by pretending to chase after a lacrosse ball. They had been playing
outside, purportedly to celebrate King George III's birthday.
When the ball was knocked over the wall into the fort, they
followed it through the open gates. Then they turned on the
soldiers in the fort and managed to capture it in minutes.

Totem

The word "totem" comes from the Ojibwa language. Everybody belonged to a totem, or clan, named after an animal or a legendary creature. People in the same totem, even if they came from different communities, considered themselves closely related.

Now Wash the Dishes...

Traditionally, in some Ojibwa communities, a groom would go to live with his bride and her family for the first years of their marriage. He would be required to perform chores for the bride and her family.

THE CREE

Remote Nomads
The Cree live in the far north of Ontario and across most of northern Canada. Today, they're the largest aboriginal nation in Canada. Traditionally, they lived mostly nomadically, hunting big game, fishing and harvesting wild rice. Because they lived so far north, the Cree didn't encounter Europeans until after most other aboriginal people in Ontario. In fact, diseases from Europe probably reached them via other aboriginal nations before they actually met the Europeans themselves.

Cultural Exchange
In the 1670s, the Hudson's Bay Company (HBC), was founded and began to establish forts across the North to trade with the Cree and the Ojibwa. Nearby Cree were divided into two groups: "homeguards," who stayed close to the forts and developed close relations with Europeans, and "uplanders," who lived nomadically in the interior. The homeguards adopted European dress and customs. The Europeans also acclimatized to the Cree way of life and sometimes married local women in Cree wedding ceremonies. The Métis people were born from these marriages.

THE LENAPE

The First New Yorkers
The Lenape (or Delaware, as Europeans called them) are originally from the New York City area. "Manhattan" is a Lenape word meaning "the island." They were displaced by Dutch and English settlers and finally pushed west to Ohio and later Oklahoma. The Munsey, a clan within the Lenape who had been converted by German missionaries to Moravianism—an obscure, pre-Reformation form of Protestantism—settled in southwestern Ontario in the 18th century.

L'ANCIEN RÉGIME

Outlaws of New France

France never got around to setting up any large-scale settlements in Ontario (partly out of fear of upsetting its aboriginal inhabitants), but French traders played a big part in the province's history. While the big companies, chartered by the French government, traded with aboriginal people from their bases in Montréal, individual settlers often travelled into the Ontario wilderness—known as the upper country, or *pays d'en haut*—to get better deals. The *coureurs des bois*, or "wood runners," were men who defied the French ban on travelling west. Like all outlaws, they had a romantic and lovable image. In Québec folklore, they are often remembered as heroes for defying authority.

Étienne Brûlé

The first—and most famous—of the *coureurs des bois* was Étienne Brûlé. Brûlé was set loose on Ontario by Samuel de Champlain, the first governor of New France, with the mission to explore and learn the language and culture of the Wendat. He did this rather too well (as far as Champlain and the Jesuits were concerned) and became completely assimilated into the Wendat. He was likely the first European to see Lake Ontario, Lake Erie, Lake Huron and Lake Superior, as well as the site of modern-day Toronto. Brûlé was a loner who had little loyalty to the French government and at times actually worked to help the English.

At age 41, his exploits finally caught up with him. He was captured by the Haudenosaunee, but managed to escape. When Brûlé returned to Huronia, the Wendat were suspicious. They figured that Brûlé had saved his own skin by agreeing to become a spy for the Haudenosaunee. Consequently, they killed him and ate him.

Voyageurs

Captured *coureurs des bois* were punished severely—the French government worried that they might reduce the profits of the companies, but more importantly, that they might start fights with aboriginal people, leading to serious political conflict. Eventually, the government decided it wasn't able to stop the *coureurs des bois*, and so started to license them in an effort to control their activities. The result was the establishment of the voyageurs, or "travellers," licenced agents of companies who ventured into the west and north to trade.

DID YOU  **KNOW?**

St. Jean de Brébeuf wrote "The Huron Carol," a Christmas song that tried to put the story of the nativity into terms that the Wendat could understand. Today, it is still commonly sung in Ontario and across Canada.

Forts

Some of Ontario's cities and towns started out as French trading forts or small settlements.

Fort Name(s)	Date of Founding	Current Name
Ste. Marie	1639	Midland
Sault Ste. Marie	1668	Sault Ste. Marie
Fort Cataraqui, later Fort Frontenac	1673	Kingston
Fort Kaninistiquia	1678	Thunder Bay
Fort St. Pierre	1731	Fort Frances
La Petite Côte	1749	Windsor
Fort Rouillé, or Fort Toronto	1750	Toronto

Ste. Marie Among the Huron

In 1639, the French Jesuits established one of their most elaborate projects: a fortified, self-sufficient mission near today's Midland, Ontario. It was the first European settlement in Ontario, built in the middle of friendly Wendat territory and far from the established French cities of Québec and Montréal. But the Jesuits managed to bring with them a cannon to defend the fort, as well as cows and sheep. The idea was to use Ste. Marie as a base for missionary work with the Wendat, and the Jesuits did manage to convert over 500 of them, though outbreaks of disease caused many Wendat to distrust the missionaries.

French Cuss

The Jesuits imagined Ste. Marie as a sort of model French town dropped into the middle of North America—useful for demonstrating the superiority of European life to the Wendat. They needed French soldiers to defend it but were concerned that the soldiers might counteract their marketing campaign and bring "the worst of Europe" with them—including drinking, swearing and womanizing.

The Canadian Martyrs

The Haudenosaunee, in their attacks on the Wendat, targeted the Jesuits, and between 1642 and 1649, eight Jesuit priests were tortured and killed. They are known as the Canadian Martyrs and were declared saints by Pope Pius XI in 1930: St. Jean de Brébeuf, St. Noël Chabanel, St. Antoine Daniel, St. Charles Garnier, St. René Goupil, St. Isaac Jogues, St. Jean de Lalande and St. Gabriel Lallement. Countless Québec churches and Catholic schools are named after them.

Ow, Ow, Ow

According to the Jesuits, the Canadian Martyrs had their ears cut off and eyes burned with coals while they were still alive. Only the bodies of Brébeuf and Lallement were recovered. The shoemaker in Ste. Marie was ordered to separate their bones from their skin and organs, which he did using a chemical solution. The bones were taken back to New France and preserved. Many Catholics today consider them to be holy relics.

Ste. Marie is Abandoned

In 1649, the remaining Jesuits decided to burn Ste. Marie rather than let it fall to the Haudenosaunee. It was never rebuilt. English settlers arrived in the area in the 1840s and the town of Midland was founded nearby in 1872. In 1940, the Jesuits again purchased the land where Ste. Marie stood. It was archeologically excavated and then reconstructed as a living museum. Pope John Paul II visited the site in 1984.

Then They Got Jobs at the Plant

Windsor started out as La Petite Côte (or "the little coast"), a farming community and satellite of the larger French settlement across the river at Fort Détroit, where modern day Detroit stands. Things didn't go well—it was later called La Côte de Misère ("the coast of misery") because the sandy soil produced poor crops. Following the American Revolution, English-speaking settlers renamed it Sandwich. The name of the original Sandwich in the UK appropriately means "sandy place" in Middle English.

The town changed its name to Windsor in the 19th century, possibly to avoid being the butt of jokes about snack food. (The original Sandwich has had no such luck, especially since one of the neighbouring towns is named Ham.)

Windsor is most famous today for being a car manufacturing centre. A small francophone population still lives there (including the family of former Prime Minister Paul Martin). They speak a unique dialect of French and trace their history back to the original colony.

DID YOU KNOW?

Baby Point in Toronto is named for the Bâby family (pronounced "Baw-bay"), francophones who moved from Windsor to Toronto and were important in early 19th century politics.

Charivari!

Ever have an urge to blackmail your neighbours for booze or money or maybe even tar and feather them? Well, you're out of luck. But if you'd been a French settler in the 18th century, you would have found the custom of "charivari" convenient. In the charivari—dating back to medieval France—local people would put on masks and harass newlyweds on their wedding night. The costumed mob would shout, sing rude songs and pelt the couple's house with rotten food. The bride and groom—no doubt eager for some privacy—would pay off the mob with money or alcohol, until they were satisfied to leave. If the newlyweds refused to hand over the goods, the mob sometimes became violent.

The charivari was later picked up by English-speaking settlers and actually hit its international height in rural Ontario in the early 19th century. It also became more violent, sometimes ending with tarring and feathering, beatings or even murder. It could be an excuse for neighbours to vent grudges or prejudices—interracial marriages or marriages between a young woman and an old man or involving a recent widow—which tended to spark violent charivaris. When the government began actively suppressing the practice, the charivari quickly died out.

THE HUDSON'S BAY COMPANY

Regarding Henry

English explorer Henry Hudson was the first European to see Hudson Bay. Like the Hudson River in New York, he gave his name to the body of water. Hudson arrived in 1610, on a mission to find the Northwest Passage. He and his crew spent the winter there. When the bay thawed in the spring, he wanted to continue on, but his crew decided they'd prefer to return to Europe. They mutinied and abandoned Hudson, his son and a few other crewmembers in a rowboat. The explorer and his group were never heard from again.

It is unclear why there was so much animosity between Hudson and his crew and why Hudson was so determined to push on at all costs along the shore of the bay. Some historians have speculated that Hudson had a secret second mission, besides the Northwest Passage, which he was bound by an oath to his backers not to reveal. This may have involved scoping out possible gold mining locations or noting sites of military value.

DID YOU KNOW?

In John Collier's famous painting *The Last Voyage of Henry Hudson*, Hudson looks depressed and hopeless, abandoned in his rowboat. (In fact, no one even knows what the explorer looked like. No portraits were ever painted of him during his lifetime.)

Many legends have surfaced about what may have happened to Hudson: that he settled on an island in the bay and died there, that he landed on the mainland and travelled almost as far south as Ottawa or that he joined a Cree community and lived there until he was very old man. So far, no evidence supports any of these legends.

From Rebels to Traitors and Back

Pierre-Esprit Radisson and his brother-in-law, Médard des Groseilliers, caused France a lot of problems. In 1659, the two settlers in New France became *coureurs des bois*, trading illegally with aboriginal people in Ontario. While travelling, they heard stories about a salty body of water to the north, which they guessed to be Hudson Bay.

When they showed up in Montréal in 1660, they were arrested, and the furs they brought were confiscated. To get even—and get rich—Radisson and des Groseilliers went to London and offered to lead a British expedition to Hudson Bay to set up trading forts there. The result: the Hudson's Bay Company, the oldest existing company in North America and, at its height, one of the most powerful corporations in the world.

Thanks for the Tip, Guys... See Ya
Radisson and des Groseilliers did not get rich. They were not given leading roles in the company and returned to France in 1674. Radisson joined the French navy and was involved in the campaign against the Hudson's Bay Company, but France continued to harass both Radisson and des Groseilliers. They were caught illegally trading again in 1683, and again, their furs were confiscated. In the end, Radisson went back to the Hudson's Bay Company and took an active role in fighting against the French. In 1687, he became an English citizen and retired in England on a small pension from the company. He was permanently banned from New France. Des Groseilliers stayed in New France.

Factory Towns

The Hudson's Bay Company was a huge help to Britain. It could get around New France and begin trading directly for furs in the north. Under the guidance of Radisson and des Groseilliers, and with the financing of Prince Rupert, they launched an expedition in 1668. The Hudson's Bay Company built its first trading post that year, at Rupert House (modern-day Waskaginish, in northern Québec). In 1673, they established Moose Factory (appropriately located on Factory Island at the mouth of the Moose River), the first British settlement in Ontario. In 1679, Fort Albany was established in northwestern Ontario. In 1684, York Factory was established in Manitoba. From there, they moved farther inland and west.

Why "factory"? Unlike modern factories, Hudson's Bay factories didn't necessarily produce anything, nor have big smokestacks. They were trading forts presided over by a "factor," an agent who bought and sold goods.

Prince Rupert of the Rhine, Poodle-Fancier

Prince Rupert loved poodles. The German-English aristocrat who financed the Hudson's Bay Company (and after whom Prince Rupert, BC, is named, as well as Rupert's Land, the territory formerly occupied by the HBC) even rode into battle with one. As general of the Royalist army during the English Civil War, he was known to go into combat with a poodle in his coat.

THE FINAL CONQUEST

A War By Any Other Name...

The war that expelled France from North America, lasted from 1754 to 1763 and goes by a few names. Americans call it the French and Indian War; the British and French call it the Seven Years' War (despite the fact that it lasted nine years!); and Québecers call it the War of the Conquest. In Ontario, it goes by either of the last two names.

The French: Toast

Most of the fighting occurred in the United States, Québec and the Atlantic provinces, but two major battles happened in Ontario: the siege of Fort Frontenac in 1758, in which Britain seized control of the fortress that later became Kingston, and the Battle of the Thousand Islands, in which Britain captured Fort Lévis on Isle Royale. By 1763, Ontario was a British possession. By 1774, modern-day southern Ontario and Québec had been formally incorporated into the British colony of Québec.

THE LOYALISTS

Loyalists and Loyalism

The Loyalists were the losers in the American Revolution. In the 1770s, they headed for the nearest safe British territory they could find—Ontario. For many years after—centuries, in fact—the legendary image of loyal subjects settling the wilderness had a way of sticking in Ontarians' imagination.

"Loyal She Began, Loyal She Remains"

Ut Incepit Fidelis Sic Permanet. This is Ontario's motto today, commemorating the role Loyalists—refugees from the United States who supported Britain during the American Revolution—played in the founding of Ontario. In fact, Ontario was mostly created for their benefit.

Your Very Own Title

United Empire Loyalists and their descendants are allowed by law to put "UE" at the end of their names. This is the only hereditary title allowed in Canada. The government has issued no other hereditary titles, and Canadians are not allowed to accept foreign titles, as Lord Conrad Black of Crossharbour (aka Conrad Black, UE) can testify. (He was forced to give up his citizenship to accept a British title.) Despite all this, almost no modern-day Ontarians put "UE" after their names. It's hardly rare enough to be special anyway—about 25 percent of Ontarians are descended, on some level, from Loyalists.

Old propaganda has a way of sticking. Britain promoted an image of Loyalists as upper class, educated, Anglo-Saxon Anglicans. "The very cream of the 13 colonies" was how Lieutenant-Governor John Graves Simcoe put it. This was almost a complete myth, especially in Ontario.

The wealthiest Loyalists mostly gave up on North America altogether and went back to England after the success of the American Revolution. Those who had lots of slaves took them to the Caribbean. Urban, middle-class Loyalists tended to go to the Maritimes, where they hoped to find more established towns and remain only a boat ride from Europe.

Those who wound up in Ontario tended to be the bottom of American society, many of them from what was then the frontier—upstate New York, Ohio, Michigan, Vermont and western Pennsylvania. There were many members of pacifist sects, such as the Mennonites and Quakers, who were distrusted in the United States because they had refused to participate in the Revolution. There were also Black Loyalists, including escaped slaves, who had joined British regiments to fight against the Americans.

DID YOU KNOW?

People often forget how many Germans came to North America. At the time of the American Revolution, they made up one-third of the population of Pennsylvania and nearly 10 percent of the total white population of all the colonies. (In surveys today, more Americans identify themselves as being German than any other ancestry.) Those who came to Ontario as Loyalists founded the city of Berlin (now Kitchener), as well as the surrounding towns of New Hamburg, Baden, Mannheim and Heidelberg. It's estimated that almost a third of all Loyalists were German-speaking.

German Names
The Loyalists gave Ontario's first districts German names: Hesse, Nassau, Mecklenburg and Lunenburg. But in the first session of Upper Canada's parliament, these were overturned and given simpler and more English names: Western, Home, Midland and Eastern.

Upper Canada:
Predecessor of the Province
(1791–1841)

An odd jumble of people settled Ontario, some with down-right wacky ideas of what the colony should be like.

It began almost unintentionally. After the Conquest, Britain didn't really know what to do with a French-speaking colony. British strategists likely had plans to trade it back to France at some future point, possibly in exchange for possessions in Europe, but that changed with the American Revolution, and later, the French Revolution. Britain wanted to hang on to whatever land it could in North America and needed a place to settle its supporters in the United States.

Out of all the muddle, large-scale settlement began in Ontario. In 1790, an act of the British parliament formally established Upper Canada, separating it from Québec (known then as Lower Canada). This way, they reasoned, an English-ruled colony could be built. By 1791, the Constitutional Act had become law.

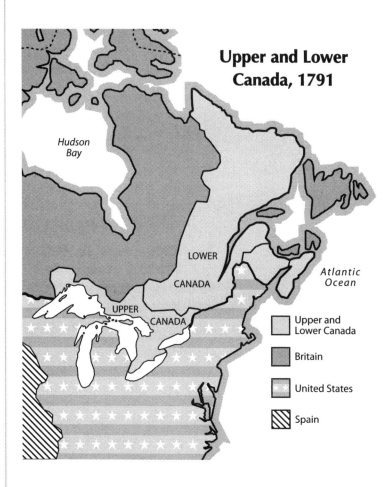

Upper and Lower Canada, 1791

Hudson Bay

Atlantic Ocean

LOWER CANADA

UPPER CANADA

Upper and Lower Canada

Britain

United States

Spain

POOF!
INSTANT COLONY

Better Late Than Never

Everyone's a winner! Loyalists were given big rewards just for showing up in Ontario. These included free land, and provisions such as seeds, farm equipment, food and clothing. Merely swearing an oath of allegiance to Britain got you 81 hectares. Soldiers who had fought for Britain, especially those who were officers, received more substantial parcels of land.

All of these bonuses induced Americans—some of whom were less than loyal—to move to Canada. This was especially true for the "late Loyalists" who came over in the next few decades to take advantage of the rewards and start a new life in Canada. Regardless of the politics of the newcomers, the government was happy to see the colony grow. By 1812, there were 90,000 Upper Canadians. Eighty percent of the population was American-born.

The Constitutional Act of 1791 set up Ontario's government:

☛ It had two houses, like the British Parliament. The upper house, with seven members, was appointed for life. The lower house, with 16 members, was elected.

☛ Only men (not including aboriginal men) could vote. They also had to be "fort-shilling freeholders," meaning owners of farms that were worth 40 shillings (or £2), annually. To give some perspective, the average British soldier at the time was paid one shilling a day—so a 40 shilling farm would be quite small.

☛ Like today, the lieutenant-governor had the power to veto bills. Unlike today, and even unlike kings in Britain at the time, he frequently used that power to overturn bills. The lieutenant-governor was assisted by his "Executive Council," a tightly knit group that he appointed and who formed the main power in the colony.

☛ Parliament met for the first time on September 17, 1792, in the Freemason's Hall in Newark (Niagara-on-the-Lake).

☛ After the capital was moved to York (or Toronto), the first parliament building was finished in 1797. The simple structure consisted of two one-storey brick buildings—the upper and lower houses—connected by a covered walkway. It stood until 1813, when invading Americans burned it down.

Two for One (Or One for Two)

Early politicians sometimes wore more than one hat. Two members of the first upper house were also on the lieutenant-governor's Executive Council. At first, most settlers were too busy to concern themselves with politics, but later they started to catch on—and get irritated by—the less-than-democratic system of government.

AN APPLE A DAY

The Apple of Ontario's Eye—McIntosh

One of Ontario's best-known contributions to agriculture is an apple cultivar given the inauspicious name of "McIntosh." It was discovered by John McIntosh, an American Loyalist who settled near the village of Dundela, near Iroquois, Ontario. In 1811, he noticed wild apple trees growing on his property and transplanted them into his garden. The origin of the trees is unknown—crabapples are the only apple species native to Ontario. Only one survived in the garden, and it produced excellent apples—which became known as McIntosh Red.

Send in the Clones

The seeds of the McIntosh did not produce the same quality of fruit, so John McIntosh set about cloning the tree by planting clippings from it. (Even today, all McIntosh apple trees are genetically identical!) By the end of the 19th century, it had become the most popular apple in the world. The original tree died in 1910, and a plaque now commemorates where it once stood.

Macintosh—the brand launched by the California-based Apple Computer—is a spelling mistake, intended to refer to the apple.

How D'Ya Like Them Apples?

Despite the hardships—a short growing season and diseases not found farther south—southern Ontario quickly became a major apple-growing region. In addition to the McIntosh, farmers began to grow Russian apple cultivars, which were adapted to cope with colder weather. The Niagara Peninsula and the north shores on Lake Ontario and Lake Erie saw the biggest apple production. In 1902, the *Brighton Ensign* reported that 1,100,621 barrels of apples were being exported from Brighton to Europe. Another 202 barrels went to Japan.

NAMING NAMES

Cobourg

The beautiful and historic town of Cobourg—once one of the fastest growing in Ontario—got its start with the not-nearly-as-nice name of Buckville. It was later renamed Amherst, and then Hamilton. It became Cobourg in 1819—a spelling mistake—named after Prince Leopold of Saxe-Coburg, who had just married Britain's Princess Charlotte. By the 1870s, Cobourg had settled into the role of a quiet resort town, catering mainly to American tourists.

Parry, Perry, Peary

Parry Sound—the great port on the rugged northeast of Georgian Bay—was named in 1822 in honour of Rear Admiral Sir William Edward Parry, an English Arctic explorer. Parry is sometimes confused with the American Arctic explorer, Rear Admiral Robert Edwin Peary. To further confound matters, Parry Sound is also sometimes confused with Port Perry, another Ontario town, located on Lake Scugog.

A Rural Colony

While the population of Upper Canada grew fast, its towns grew slowly. In 1812, York had a population of only 700.

A Gay Old Time

It's hard to know what York settler Alexander Wood would have thought of his current reputation—as presiding gay martyr and patron of Toronto's Gay Village. A merchant and magistrate from Scotland, Wood was banished from Ontario after inspecting the genitals of several men—he claimed it was to gather information for a case he was investigating. Wood returned to Toronto in 1812, and managed to clear his name. Alexander Street and Wood Street in the Gay Village are named after him. A statue of him was recently built.

JOHN GRAVES SIMCOE AND HIS PALS:
GUYS WITH SOME FUNNY IDEAS

Simcoe

Upper Canada's first lieutenant-governor was John Graves Simcoe, an eccentric Eton and Oxford-educated English army officer. He showed up in Ontario in 1792, and immediately set to work trying to create a miniature duplicate of England in the wilderness. Simcoe's personality seems to have been a mix of conservative politics and an almost boyish enthusiasm for pursuing schemes.

He had been one of the most successful British commanding officers in the American Revolution (though he probably regretted ordering his men to stop shooting retreating Americans in the back after the Battle of Brandywine, as one of those Americans turned out to be George Washington).

Loose Lips Sink Ships
Sensibly, Simcoe decided that the provincial capital, Newark (now called Niagara-on-the-Lake), founded 11 years earlier by Loyalists, was too close to the American border. This was not a hard decision to make—the American-held Fort Niagara, across the Niagara River, was within shouting distance!

Not too many Ontario residents know the official name given to the August civic holiday in Ontario—Simcoe Day. But do you really need an excuse for a day off? In Toronto, it's better known as Caribana weekend, after the massive Caribbean carnival that is the biggest street party in North America.

London Calling

As a new capital, Simcoe decided to found London—a city that he imagined would eventually be like the original London in every way. To start work on this goal, he ordered that the Askunessippi River be renamed the Thames River. Unfortunately (for Simcoe at least), his boss and archrival, the governor of Upper and Lower Canada, Lord Dorchester, rejected London as the capital.

In fact, Dorchester and Simcoe never got along—Dorchester had wanted Sir John Johnson (Second Baronet of New York) as lieutenant-governor. Johnson was part of an established British North American family, with blood connections to the politically important Mohawk.

The Grand Old Duke of York

Simcoe's second choice for a capital was approved by Lord Dorchester and founded in 1793. Simcoe named it York after the extremely unsuccessful military leader Prince Frederick, Duke of York (naming major locations on whims, and after personal friends, seems to have been Simcoe's habit). Frederick had the dubious distinction of being the favourite son of King George III (who was less than sane, even on his good days, and was a notoriously bad decision maker). Fredericton, New Brunswick is also named after him, and he was the inspiration for a popular nursery rhyme:

> *The grand old Duke of York,*
> *He had ten thousand men.*
> *He marched them up to the top of the hill*
> *And he marched them down again.*
> *And when they were up, they were up.*
> *And when they were down, they were down.*
> *And when they were only halfway up,*
> *They were neither up nor down.*

Frederick found himself in trouble later on when his mistress, Mary Anne Clarke, was accused of making a profit by offering up for sale officers' positions in the army (using the influence of Frederick) to wealthy civilians with no military training. Regardless, Parliament voted to exonerate Frederick of any wrongdoing.

DID YOU  KNOW?

Coincidentally, Clarke was the great-grandmother of the famous actor Sir Gerald du Maurier, for whom Canada's Du Maurier brand of cigarettes is named.

Toronto Harbour—Kind of Like the Mediterranean?

York Harbour was partly surrounded by a sandbar peninsula (which would later break off and become the Toronto Islands). Simcoe had the idea that the sandbar would protect the harbour and the town and keep it safe from naval attack. The key point, at least as Simcoe saw it, was that the end of the peninsula controlled access to Toronto in the same way that Gibraltar controlled entry to the Mediterranean Sea. This slightly grandiose comparison led Simcoe to actually name it Gibraltar Point, as it's still called, and build a military blockhouse there. Officers at Fort York were skeptical of this logic—with good reason. During the War of 1812, the Americans simply landed farther down the coast and walked into Toronto, which surrendered to them.

DID YOU KNOW?

Simcoe was many things, but not shy when it came to self-promotion. He named Lake Simcoe after his father, Captain John Simcoe (though cynics began to claim, almost immediately, that he had really named it after himself).

Upper Canada, Slavery-Free

Simcoe clashed constantly with the elected legislature, which was mostly made up of poorly educated, lower middle-class American immigrants. Although they officially supported the king, they had no interest in recreating English society and its hierarchies. On the other hand, they, unlike Simcoe, supported slavery. Some settlers even brought slaves with them from the United States. Simcoe convinced them to pass a law banning the importation of new slaves into Ontario and freeing all slave children when they reached the age of 25. This completely ended slavery in Ontario by 1810, 23 years before it was banned in the rest of the British Empire.

Simcoe's Wife

The oddly named Elizabeth Posthuma Gwillim-Simcoe, Simcoe's wife, was famous for her diaries and watercolour land-scapes of early colonial Ontario. Simcoe named the towns of East Gwillimbury and Bradford-West Gwillimbury after his wife. Elizabeth's father was an aide-de-camp to General James Wolfe during the British siege of Québec, and her mother died during her birth. In a weird example of taste, she was named Posthuma in memory of her dead mother.

 Soldiers tend to make bad politicians, but if they do one thing well in office, it's building and maintaining roads. Simcoe knew the value of roads for moving troops and sup-plies, and one of his biggest achievements in Ontario was road construction.

The longest was Kingston Road, later known as Highway 2, connecting York and Kingston along the north shore of Lake Ontario. The work was contracted to a firm owned by an American, "Colonel" Asa Danforth (he had never actually been in the army). Danforth accused the government of cheating him on payment for the road and withholding grants of free land that it had promised to his workers. For its part, the government blamed Danforth for being incompetent, since bridges collapsed and parts of the road quickly washed out. Danforth was angry enough to leave the country and even try, temporarily, to arrange a rebellion to overthrow the government of Upper Canada. His scheme didn't pan out, but his name did stick to Danforth Road in Scarborough, and later to Danforth Avenue in Toronto.

Dundas Done Wrong

Simcoe also had Dundas Street built, connecting York to Dundas (near Hamilton). Simcoe hoped to continue the road all the way to London, maybe still clinging to the idea of moving the capital there. The street and town of Dundas are named after Simcoe's friend Henry Dundas (First Viscount Melville), a Scottish politician. Dundas at one point headed the British navy, but was impeached for financial mismanagement.

Yonge Street is probably the best known of Simcoe's roads, built over drained marshes, in what was then the west end of York. The street takes its name from another of Simcoe's pals, Sir George Yonge (Fifth Baronet of Culliton), the British Secretary of War at the time. Neither Dundas nor Yonge ever visited Toronto.

Gambler in Command

In 1796, Simcoe became sick and went back to England to recuperate. Peter Russell, a compulsive gambler, whose career was mostly dictated by his need to take whatever jobs he could get to cover debts, temporarily replaced him. Unable to get work in England, he became an officer in the American Revolutionary War and later (amazingly) a judge in Upper Canada. By 1799, Simcoe had decided not to return, and Russell was replaced. Russell's main talent—since he was an unsuccessful gambler and mediocre politician—seems to have been collecting land. He used his influence to transfer huge tracts into his own name.

Castle Frank, Not Castle Frankenstein

Simcoe built a house for himself on a hill outside of York and called it Castle Frank. It was accidentally burned down by fishermen in 1829 and is now the site of the Castle Frank subway station.

TORONTO

Taronto

The French called Lake Simcoe *Lac des Claies* ("Lake of Weirs," referring to the traps that aboriginal people used to catch fish) or *Lac Taronto* (probably the Mohawk word *tkaronto*, meaning "where there are trees standing in the water"). The name Taronto (later spelled Toronto) spread south to Lake Ontario along the old Wendat trading route known as *le passage de Taronto*. At its southern end was a river known as Rivière Taronto, which Simcoe renamed the Humber River.

From York to Toronto
The name Taronto made a comeback in 1834, when York incorporated as a city and was renamed Toronto. Mississauga was originally known as Toronto Township and part of modern-day Brampton, northwest of Toronto, was called Toronto-Gore Township. Many other theories about the origins of Toronto's name—the most popular one being that it comes from a Wendat word meaning "meeting place"—have been discredited by historians. Another rumour, with even less truth to it, is that an early Italian settler named Toronto after Tarento, Italy.

One of Many

Toronto had to beat out other challengers for its name. Erindale—part of modern-day Mississauga—was originally named Toronto in 1830. It was changed to Springfield shortly afterwards and eventually to Erindale in 1900. Cooksville, in Mississauga, might also have been called Toronto—the name that its post office was originally given. The same applies to Port Hope.

The spelling of Toronto with an "o" instead of an "a" seems to go back to French maps. Strangely, though, most people pronounce it the old way, *Tah-ronto*, rather than *Tow-ronto*.

AND THE LAND GOES TO...

"King" Talbot

Part of Simcoe's scheme to duplicate England involved selling huge parcels of land, including whole townships, to trusted friends, who could then lease it out to tenants. Simcoe hoped that this would create an unofficial aristocracy. Colonel Thomas Talbot, Simcoe's private secretary, was in charge of a fiefdom of 263 km² on the north shore of Lake Erie, today spanning six counties. Talbot considered himself patriarch of his tiny kingdom. New settlers apparently had their names marked on land maps in pencil—and would have their ownership erased if they offended Talbot. He imposed his own rules on the settlers, forcing them to build roads or public buildings and carry out other tasks for him. Talbot himself lived in a mansion in the village of Port Talbot, which he had named after himself. During the War of 1812, the Americans raided the village (with the help of some of Talbot's disgruntled subjects). The despot narrowly escaped being captured by running out one door of his house as the Americans ran in the other. The town of Talbotville and (even more audaciously) the city of St. Thomas are also named for him.

Less-than-Pure Intentions

The wealthy men such as Talbot who coordinated the settlements had more than the prestige of leadership to motivate them. The government entered into agreements to offer free land to them in exchange for encouraging settlement. Naturally, these men took the best land for themselves—at no cost—while leasing or selling poor quality land to settlers. Thomas Douglas, Fifth Earl of Selkirk (better known in Canada as Lord Selkirk), experimented with a colony in Ontario in 1802, before launching his

more successful Red River colony in Manitoba. He received
60 hectares of land for every person that he helped settle into
a disastrously swampy property named Baldoon, near Chatham.

The Baldoon Mystery

As a major settlement, Baldoon failed almost immediately. But
as a piece of mystery and folklore, it has had a successful after-
life. One determined settler who allegedly decided to stick it out
after arriving on his land was John McDonald. In 1804, he and
his wife built a house and barn there. They had a strange neighbour—an unsociable old woman who lived in a long, low log
house. Almost immediately, according to legend, a variety of
supernatural forces assaulted the McDonald family. Beams fell
out of the ceiling of their barn and bullets flew into their house
from nowhere, smashing the windows and passing through the
walls without leaving a mark. Strange noises were heard, and in
the kitchen, cups and saucers sailed through the air. Flames and
pouring water also appeared spontaneously.

The McDonald family temporarily abandoned their house and sought the help of a psychic. She told them that the culprit was none other than their mysterious neighbour. John McDonald had earlier refused to sell the old woman part of his property. According to the psychic, the woman spied on the McDonalds by turning herself into a goose. McDonald agreed that he had seen a strange goose walking around on his land. Following the psychic's advice and using a silver bullet, he shot the goose in the wing. It cried out like a human and hobbled away. Soon after, McDonald went to see the old woman. She had a broken arm and the strange occurrences immediately ceased.

Clergy Reserves

Under the laws imposed in Ontario by the British Parliament, one-seventh of all land was to be given to the Church (and by this, it meant the Anglican Church, though the Presbyterian Church was later allowed to benefit). This became a major sore spot for settlers of other denominations.

One of the biggest critics of the clergy reserves was Rev. Dr. Adolphus Egerton Ryerson, a Loyalist Anglican who had converted to Methodism. Ryerson went on to found the public school system in Ontario, on which school systems in the rest of Canada are based. He also founded Victoria College, which later merged with the University of Toronto. Long after his death, Ryerson University was named in his honour.

DID YOU KNOW?

During Upper Canada's early days, the colony was run by a small clique—mostly from Britain and mostly with authoritarian attitudes that differed from Loyalist Americans. In addition to their opposition to representative democracy, they also advocated a kind of Anglican theocracy.

Bishop John Astrakhan (pronounced "Strawn") was one of the leading members of this group, sometimes called the "Family Compact" because it was made up of a few powerful families. Astrakhan was a Scottish-born Anglican clergyman and teacher, based mostly in York. He wrote a book that was sold in Britain, which tried to convince more British citizens to immigrate to Upper Canada, but added that "levellers and democrats" were not welcome and would find "no kindred spirits here." An incredibly stubborn and remarkably energetic man, Astrakhan spent most of his life in Upper Canada advocating ultra-conservative politics and ultra-Anglican religious beliefs. Lord Elgin called him "the most dangerous and spiteful man in Upper Canada."

Anarchy in the U.S.

Astrakhan pushed to have universities built in Canada, because "those sent to the United States commonly learn little beyond anarchy in politics and infidelity in religion."

He went on to help found King's College, the precursor to the University of Toronto. When the university became secularized— or "godless," as Astrakhan put it—he started Trinity College, a specifically Anglican university. Trinity later joined the U of T as an affiliate college. Its original campus is now Trinity-Bellwoods Park in Toronto. Only its gates, commemorating Astrakhan, remain, appropriately located at the corner of Queen and Astrakhan Streets.

St. George

Although most Europeans considered Upper Canada a backwater, it did attract a few exotic exiles. The French aristocrat Laurent Quetton St. George built a lavish house in York in 1811. He escaped from France after the French Revolution and arrived in England on April 23—St. George's Day. He added "St. George" (the patron saint of England) to his name because of this. St. George Street, St. George Subway Station and the University of Toronto's St. George Campus are all named after him.

JOSEPH BRANT:
A CHIEF SO NICE,
THEY NAMED HIM TWICE

Tyendinaga, aka Joseph Brant

Europeans only accidentally came to know the famous Mohawk leader Tyendinaga as Joseph Brant. His stepfather, Carrihago, also went by the Christian name of Bernard. Tyendinaga was sent to a Christian school and given the name Joseph. English friends started calling him Bernard's Joseph, and this eventually became switched around and corrupted to Joseph Brant. Tyendinaga means "two sticks of wood bound together for strength." He was said to be descended from Wendat prisoners assimilated into the Mohawk a century earlier. Today, Brant's English name is honoured by the city of Brantford and Brant County, while the Tyendinaga Reserve near Belleville pays tribute to his Mohawk name.

Family Ties

Brant adopted many European customs and became a strong supporter of Britain, partly because of his friendship with his brother-in-law, Sir William Johnson. Johnson married Brant's older sister Mary (also known as Molly, and in Mohawk as Konwatsi'tsiaiénni). Mary was a clan mother and considered by the Mohawk to be a much more important figure than Joseph. The famous poet Pauline Johnson was the great-great-great-granddaughter of Mary. Sir William Johnson was made Baronet of New York—and his descendants (from his first marriage, to a German woman) still use the title.

Gotcha!

Some say that Mary Brant first attracted William's attention by jumping off a moving horse onto his back and clinging to him as the animal ran around the field. It seemed to work—they had their first child in the same year that Johnson's first wife died. They were married in a Mohawk ceremony that was never accepted as legal by European authorities, though they both saw it as official.

Brant Comes to Canada

Brant was born near modern-day Akron, Ohio, in the traditional territory of the Haudenosaunee. He fought successfully on the British side of the American Revolutionary War and won a lot of territory for Britain on the western frontier. Unfortunately, the Haudanosaunee's British allies let them down and managed to lose the main part of the war on the East Coast. Britain surrendered the Haudanosaunee's homeland to the Americans, though the Six Nations hadn't considered themselves to have been under British rule.

Unfortunately, they had little say in the matter—especially after 1779, when the Americans burned 41 of their towns. As a result, Brant was forced to become a refugee and grudgingly settled for the land Britain offered him in Ontario. He helped establish the territory that became the Six Nations of the Grand River Reserve, now the most populous reserve in Canada.

The Haudenosaunee Nation was originally promised 10 kilometres of land on either side of the Grand River, from Lake Erie to its source in the Niagara Escarpment. They ultimately lost most of the territory through some initial sales made by Brant, and long after his death, through a controversial land grab made by the government before Confederation.

Sorry, I Don't Swing that Way
In 1776, when Joseph Brant visited King George III at his palace, he was shocked to see grown men kissing the king's hand. He refused to do the same, explaining that he would not kiss the hand of any man, but he would be happy to kiss the queen's hand.

A Handy Gift

Brant was given ceremonial pistols and a rifle as a gift from the king. These came in handy on the trip back, when American privateers attacked his ship. Brant and his cousin John Desoronto shot five of the Americans before they fled.

DID YOU KNOW?

Brant always wore a gold ring on which he had inscribed "J. Brant – Tyendinaga." If he died in battle, he hoped that this would make his body easy to identify.

Family Violence

Brant and his eldest son, Isaac, never got along. At one point, Isaac attacked his father with a knife, badly cutting the back of his hand. Brant struck Isaac back with a dagger, cutting his head. Brant had Isaac bandaged by a doctor, but his son tore the dressings off, and a few days later he died of infection.

Rattlesnake Stew
During the American Revolutionary War, Joseph Brant became sick with a fever. He claimed to have cured it in the traditional way: by catching a rattlesnake, boiling it and drinking the broth.

THE WAR OF 1812:
THE LONGEST YEAR

It Felt Like a Year!

Time goes fast when you're having fun. Does it also go fast when you're having your house and crops burned? Despite its name, the War of 1812 lasted two and a half years, from June 18, 1812, to Christmas Eve, 1814. Most of the fighting actually happened in 1813 and 1814.

The 1812 Overture

As surprising as it may be to Canadians (and Americans), Tchaikovsky's *1812 Overture* is not about the War of 1812. It's actually about Napoleon's failed invasion of Russia, which happened in the same year. Nevertheless, it still gets treated as a patriotic piece of music in the U.S. today. Because the War of 1812 happened at the same time as the Napoleonic War, some historians don't consider it a separate war at all, but just a different theatre of battle.

Everyone's a Winner!

Who won the War of 1812? Anyone who had to sit (awake) through Canadian high school history classes would probably say Canada—despite the fact that Canada did not yet exist. On the other hand, the Americans claim they won, though they generally pay much less attention to the war. In Britain, the war is barely remembered at all.

In fact, no one won the war. British and Canadian forces kept the Americans out of Canada, but counterattacks into the United States were also defeated. In the end, the Treaty of Ghent restored things to almost exactly as they were before the war.

The Problem with Relying on Polls...

U.S. President James Madison took a pro-war position because most of his supporters did. Of course, he also went with his supporters on the issue of raising taxes—they were opposed to it. The result was that the U.S. could not afford an army or navy large enough to fight the war effectively.

New England for Old England?

In the U.S., the war's supporters came mostly from the south and west of the country. In New York and New England, people were afraid that the war would harm their shipping businesses. New England politicians voted against the war, sold food to the British army, gave Britain loans and refused to allow their state militia to fight in the war.

Myth 1: The Upper Canada Militia

Despite the heroic propaganda put out by the Upper Canada government after the war, local militiamen didn't have much of a role in the fighting. British regular troops and their First Nations allies carried out almost all of the battles.

But the militia was important to Upper Canada. Many of the American-born settlers started out being unconcerned about whether the colony was under British or American rule. But when militiamen started being shot at, they took on a much more anti-American position. This memory filtered across the province and became a central part of Ontario's identity.

Intelligence Problems

The American government went into the war with wildly optimistic information on the Canadian forces. An 1812 report by the Secretary of War, William Eustis, said that the Canadian militia were "the meanest among the refuse of men…trained only in drunken frolics on common week days." The British army in Canada, for its part, was "much debilitated by intemperance." Actually, there may have been some truth to the first rumour. The British authorities themselves considered only 4000 out of the 11,000 Upper Canadian militia troops to be reliable and loyal. The Americans were mistaken, though, in President Madison's claim that conquering Upper Canada would be a "mere matter of marching."

Unsung Heroes

When the war started, there were only 1600 regular British soldiers in Upper Canada. These men—mostly poor youth—and the government's aboriginal allies, are principally responsible for the existence of Ontario (and probably Canada) today.

Myth 2: Major General Brock, Canadian

Major General Sir Isaac Brock, Hero of Upper Canada (the title officially bestowed on him) didn't really like Canada nor have any interest in it. Like all British officers, he wanted to be in Europe, fighting Napoleon. Also, like all (or at least, most) British officers, he distrusted Canadians and the Canadian militia.

Brock became both commander of the military and head of the civilian government in Upper Canada. He managed to impress almost everyone he met. Aside from his personality, he stood nearly 2 metres in height (in sharp contrast to his friend and ally, Tecumseh, who was known for his unusually short stature).

Tecumseh

One of the most prominent figures of the war was Tecumseh, a Shawnee chief who fought with Britain. He had been fighting the Americans before the war started, nearly his whole life, in fact, as settlers began to encroach on his home in Ohio. Tecumseh led an alliance of people from various nations and was crucial in helping Brock capture Detroit. If they won the war, Brock promised to give Tecumseh modern-day Michigan and recognize it as a sovereign aboriginal state. Unfortunately, though, the advancing American army killed Tecumseh at Moraviantown (near London, Ontario) the next year in the Battle of the Thames.

A Good Head for the Situation

Brock complained about being unable to find a hat big enough to fit his head in Upper Canada and had to have one specially ordered from Britain.

What Qualifications?

Despite not actually being a Canadian, Brock was voted the 28th greatest Canadian in a vote held in 2004 by the Canadian Broadcasting Corporation (CBC). Tecumseh—also not a Canadian—finished in 37th place.

Death

Brock was undoubtedly brave, though possibly a bit reckless. His philosophy was that he must never ask men to go where he would not dare to lead them. On October 3, 1812, while in full uniform (which clearly identified him to the enemy), he led a charge against invading Americans at Queenston Heights, near Niagara Falls. The result was—predictably— bad for Brock. After Brock's death, much less competent officers replaced him, and the war went downhill from Canada's perspective.

Or Was it Just "Ow"?

What were Brock's last words? A stone marker at Queenston Heights (not far from the massive Brock Monument) says it was "*Surgite!*" (Latin for "press on"). It's hard to imagine that any of his men would have known what this meant, though. The traditional folksong, the *Ballad of Queenston Heights*, says that they were "Push on, York volunteers!" Still other sources claim they were the absurdly wordy "May my fall not be noticed or impede my brave companions from advancing to victory." Contradictory reports also say that he died instantly and had nothing to say.

NOT A MYTH, BUT A REAL WOMAN

Laura Secord

The great heroine of the War of 1812 was Laura Secord. When American troops overran Queenston, she was forced to billet several soldiers in her house. She heard them talking about a surprise attack that was being planned at Beaver Dams (near modern-day Thorold) and walked over 32 kilometres, an 18-hour journey, to warn the British commander. The resulting battle was a total victory for Britain.

What, No Chocolates, Even?

Secord lived to the age of 93. The Upper Canada government never rewarded her for her work during the war. In 1860, Albert Edward, Prince of Wales, heard her story during his tour of Canada and sent her £100 in gold.

The Laura Secord Chocolate Company, started in 1933, has used several images of young women on its logos over the years. None of them are the actual Secord (she was 37, considerably older than the woman in the images, during the War of 1812). No portraits were made of Secord until much later in her life.

Canada's Paul Reveres?

Secord has sometimes been called "Canada's Paul Revere," comparing her to the hero of the American Revolutionary War. The same phrase has been used for Billy Green, a local boy who rushed to report the position of American troops to the British command. He was able to guide British forces into a surprise attack in the Battle of Stoney Creek, expelling the Americans from the Niagara Peninsula.

BURNINGS AND BATTLES

Burning of Toronto

On April 27, 1813, the American navy attacked York and landed soldiers there. The British army abandoned the town but first blew up the arms depot at Fort York. The explosion was unexpectedly huge and killed American Brigadier General Zebulon Pike and 38 American soldiers. The Americans occupied York for six days, and looted and burned much of the town, including the parliament buildings. Bishop John Astrakhan, for his part, negotiated the surrender of York and acted as its de facto protector during the week of the occupation, making himself as annoying as possible with a constant series of petitions and complaints to the American commanders.

Burning of Washington

Britain got revenge for the burning of York and other towns in Upper Canada, though no Canadians took part in the project. Between August 17 and 28, 1814, British ships fought their way into Chesapeake Bay, landed troops and attacked Washington, DC. The city was barely defended (government officials had run away), and many public buildings, including the president's house, were torched. Later, when the house was being repaired, it was whitewashed to cover the burn marks and so became known as the "White House." Baltimore was also bombarded. John Astrakhan endorsed these controversial attacks as fair treatment considering what his town of York had faced.

Battle of New Orleans

In January 1815—after peace had been declared—a British force in the Caribbean, which had not yet heard that the war was over, attacked New Orleans. The Britons were badly defeated by the American army under Andrew Jackson, who later used the fame he gained from the battle to successfully run for president. In the U.S., this is the best-remembered battle of the war. In Canada, it is probably the least remembered.

RESTLESS YEARS

The Bloody Assize

With the war over, attention turned to those who had assisted the American invaders. Eight men were hanged and seven were banished from the province in what was called the "Bloody Assize." The name was a reference to the (even bloodier) reprisals that took place after a 17th century uprising in England. Others who had helped the Americans faced harassment and reprisals from their pro-British neighbours.

Qualifications… Pah!

John Beverley Robinson became Upper Canada's attorney general in 1812, despite the fact that he was only 21 years old and not yet a lawyer. Unconfirmed rumours implied that his appointment was helped by the fact that he was dating the daughter of the chief justice.

Good Doggie… Here's a Township

In the 1820s, Lieutenant-Governor Sir Peregrine Maitland named the townships of Tiny, Tay and Flos (in Simcoe County) after his wife's three poodles.

It's a Beaut!

In 1816, small, hamlet-sounding Meyers Creek got the pretty new name of Belleville. It was named after Arabella Gore, the wife of Lieutenant-Governor Francis Gore.

Public? Private? What's the Difference?

In 1821, the Bank of Upper Canada—the colony's first bank— was founded in York. Its president was William Allen, at that time the wealthiest man in York and a central member of the ruling clique, the Family Compact.

Gourlay's Questionnaires

One of the first challenges to the ruling elite of Upper Canada came from Robert Gourlay (not to be confused with 20th-century crooner Robert Goulet!).

Gourlay arrived from Scotland in 1817 and got approval from the government to analyze immigration and settlement systems. He issued a questionnaire to all the landowners in the province to seek their opinions regarding settlement policies. The responses were mostly negative. People complained that there were too few settlers because of the government's refusal to allow any more Americans into Upper Canada. The government was also blamed for holding back development by refusing to sell or build on clergy reserves and on land personally owned by government officials. The responses seem to have set Gourlay himself into a frenzy of anger at the government.

In 1818, Gourlay put out a second letter to landowners. Instead of a questionnaire, this one was a rambling diatribe against the ruling elite, asking for landowners to support an inquiry into the government's policies and structure. He then sent out a third letter, calling for community meetings to elect petitioners who would go to London to represent the colony, circumventing the Upper Canada legislature.

That was it for Gourlay. The government had him hauled in front of a panel of magistrates, charged under the Seditions Act (which was really meant to keep Irish rebels out of Upper Canada) and deported to Scotland.

Just Ignore the Political Record…
In 1821, a non-Loyalist American, Barnabas Bidwell was elected to the legislative assembly. He had been attorney general of Massachusetts, but had come to Upper Canada to avoid trial for misusing public funds. His election was rejected by the legislature, but his son ran in his place, won and was accepted.

EARLY ON

Welcome to the Force... By Force

Early Toronto had trouble finding police officers to patrol its streets. The province started randomly ordering citizens to become police constables on a temporary basis. Several residents were fined considerable amounts for refusing to serve on the force.

Pay for Your Room, or I'm Taking You In

Crime was so widespread in 19th-century Ontario that the government ordered that every innkeeper be deputized as a constable. From 1823 to as late as 1887, this law stayed in place. Innkeepers turned out to be more than willing to use (and sometimes abuse) their newfound power.

Bouncing Back

In 1831, Scottish newspaper publisher William Lyon Mackenzie was elected to the legislature, but he was expelled almost immediately after being accused of slandering the assembly in his newspaper, *The Colonial Advocate*. He ran in a by-election and was re-elected, only to be expelled again. This went on five times before he gave up and switched jobs, becoming the first mayor of Toronto.

DID YOU KNOW?

Duelling pays—at least when you're on the winning side. The last recorded duel in Ontario happened on June 13, 1833, near Perth (today, the pistols used are on display in the Perth Museum). Two friends, John Wilson and Robert Lyon, fought over a woman, Elizabeth Hughes. Lyon was killed, and Wilson was acquitted of murder on the grounds that it was Lyon who had pushed for the duel and that Wilson had shown remorse for killing his friend. He later married Hughes and became a criminal defence lawyer.

Upper Canadian Democracy

Democracy was a relative term in Upper Canadian politics before the reforms that followed the 1837 Rebellion. Secret ballots (originally called "Australian ballots" because they were first used in Tasmania in 1856) were not yet in use. Only a coward or a criminal would want to hide his political choices from scrutiny, it was argued. Voters had to stand before an assembled crowd in the voting office and announce their selection. If they made the "wrong" choice, armed thugs often awaited the voter down the street. In fact, if both candidates had hired thugs, voters might get a clubbing either way. Threats and bribes of alcohol and money were a major factor in politics. Not surprisingly, most people decided to stay away entirely. Voter turnout, even from the small pool of eligible voters, was low.

Cheap Booze

Upper Canadians were relative masters of restraint—"relative" being the operative word. Upper Canada "may be pronounced the most healthy country under the sun, considering that whiskey can be procured for about one shilling sterling per gallon," said the Huron Tract developer, William "Tiger" Dunlop.

Painful Protest
The village of York became incorporated as the town of Toronto in 1834. That year also saw one of the Toronto's most bizarre accidents.

Imagine this scene: Mackenzie, mayor of Toronto, is giving one of his trademark fiery speeches in the council hall. The hall is on the second floor of the St. Lawrence Market, with butchers' stalls below. Mackenzie's detractors pack the hall and start stamping their feet in unison. Suddenly, the floor gives way, and half of the gallery falls through to the first floor. Twenty-four people are seriously injured and three die after being impaled on meat hooks.

 Kingston Penitentiary was built in 1835 as the provincial prison of Upper Canada. It is one of the world's oldest jails still in use.

- ☞ Inmates in Kingston Pen sewed the original uniforms used by the North-West Mounted Police (who became the RCMP). They also forged some of the metalwork used in the parliamentary library in Ottawa.

- ☞ What did Victorian thrill-seekers do? In the 19th century, the jail attracted tourists and even charged them admission to come inside and see the prisoners.

- ☞ The first inmate in the Kingston Pen was Joseph Bouchette of Northumberland County. He was sentenced to five years for grand larceny on January 14, 1835.

- ☞ In 1878, Sara Jane Pierce, a nine-year-old girl, was sentenced to seven years in the prison for breaking and entering and larceny. She was found guilty of stealing a quilt, a hat, a towel and a few handfuls of food.

- ☞ The prison's youngest inmate was eight-year-old Antoine Beauche of Québec City. He was sentenced to three years for pickpocketing while aboard a ship in the St. Lawrence. The boy was whipped 47 times in his first nine months in prison. The reason? For such reprehensible behaviour as staring, laughing, whistling and idling.

- ☞ At least 50 people have successfully escaped from the prison in 26 jailbreaks—the first in 1836. The latest person to do it was (the appropriately named) Ty Conn, who scaled the wall in 1999. He made it to Toronto, but died in his hideout after shooting himself during a telephone interview with a reporter.

Bond Head, Bone Head

In 1836, Britain sent Sir Francis Bond Head to become lieutenant-governor of Upper Canada. He did not calm the tensions in the colony, challenging the opponents of the government: "Let them come if they dare!" He teased the rebels further, showing how confident he was that they would be defeated by moving the troops stationed in Upper Canada into Lower Canada to help deal with the rebellion there. Bond Head did have his fans. Two towns in Ontario are named Bond Head after him, as is Bond Street in Toronto (a street that, ironically, would later be home to William Lyon Mackenzie).

Upper Canada Loses Its Head

Bond Head's mistakes caused him to lose his job. He was recalled to England in 1838 and had to make the trip through New York City. A legend says that he passed through Rochester, New York—very unfriendly territory—and actually stayed at the same hotel as Mackenzie, now in exile. Bond Head felt obliged to disguise himself as a servant, but Mackenzie recognized him, and—ever unpredictable—laughed and greeted him in a friendly way.

MAKING ITS MARK

First Pitch?

The first recorded game of baseball in Canada—and possibly the first game of modern baseball in the world—happened on June 4, 1838, in Beachville, south of London. That's a full year before Abner Doubleday officially invented baseball in Cooperstown, New York. Most modern historians, though, believe that the game dates back much further than either event. Primordial stick and ball games in North America and Europe go back at least 100 years earlier. So when did baseball become baseball? That's one question that sports historians still can't answer.

Tough Gals

Far from Britain, women felt less restrained by rigid rules governing how they should act. The English naturalist Charles Fothergill whined, after a trip to an Upper Canadian pub, about "decent and even pretty girls hawking and spitting around the room, occasionally scratching and rubbing themselves and lounging in attitudes in their chairs in a way that in Britain would be unpardonable."

The Passenger Pigeon

Wild Passenger Pigeons once darkened the skies of Upper Canada, flying in flocks of thousands, sometimes in clouds stretching kilometres. To settlers, shooting pigeons was a welcome sport and a source of food. Alas, the massive flocks were not inexhaustible; the birds had disappeared from the skies by the end of the 19th century. The last passenger pigeon died in 1914 in the Cincinnati Zoo. Today, a few stuffed pigeons in Ontario museums are the only reminders that the bird ever existed.

Funny Money

In early 19th century Ontario, private banks printed their own money, often in odd denominations ($3 or $4). Bills were signed by bank presidents to prove their authenticity. Banks needed to keep enough gold on hand to redeem the bills when customers returned them (or if they became uncomfortable with the sketchiness of a particular bank's currency). Ontarians were apparently a trusting bunch; they preferred to hoard their bills rather than rush the bank.

This Way, Please

The British consul in New York, James Buchanan, actually took it upon himself to redirect protestant Irish immigrants to Upper Canada. He arranged to meet the immigrant boats in the harbour and offered their passengers land in the Port Hope area.

Literary Pioneers

In the 1820s and 1830s, Upper Canada had its first literary pioneers—literally. These authors, from upper-class British backgrounds, became the first people to write extensively about daily life in Upper Canada. Two families are the best known: the siblings Samuel Strickland, Susannah Moodie and Catharine Parr Traill, and the siblings John Langton and Anne Langton. Most of what we know today about pioneer life comes from these writers.

Underground Railroad

Between 1810 and 1850, about 20,000 escaped black slaves made it to Ontario from the United States. The escaped slaves, mainly young men, were sometimes able to buy the freedom of their families and have them legally moved north. About 1000 settled in Toronto, while the rest set up in rural areas, particularly in southwestern of Ontario. Conditions were harsh—the weather was colder than what the new immigrants were used to, and the government and their white neighbours were often hostile. After slavery ended in the U.S., many black Ontarians returned to their home country, but others stayed.

DID YOU KNOW?

Buxton, a village near Chatham in Kent County, was founded in 1849 by escaped slaves who secured their own township with land bought from the government. The town boomed, and after paying off their debts, the settlers had enough money left to send their children to school, producing a generation of successful black professionals. Seventy men from Buxton joined the North during the American Civil War. Two black doctors from Buxton set up the first hospital for blacks in the U.S. Dr. Anderson Abbott, an escaped slave, became a coroner for Kent County and president of the Chatham Medical Society as well as the Chatham Literary and Debating Society.

Mary Ann Shadd Carey

The Underground Railroad was promoted through the *Provincial Freeman*, a newspaper launched in 1853 to serve the local black community. It became famous as the world's first newspaper edited by a woman, Mary Ann Shadd Carey—an escaped slave herself.

The Real McCoy?

One of the theories about how the phrase "the real McCoy" got its start credits the famous black inventor, Elijah McCoy. McCoy invented a new lubrication system for steam engines, which turned out to be so popular (and frequently imitated) that his customers demanded "the real McCoy." McCoy was born in Essex County, Ontario, in 1884, the son of escaped slaves. While still young, his family moved to Detroit. He also invented the folding ironing board and the lawn sprinkler.

AND COMMUNITIES WERE BORN

Circular Cities

Some early planners were bored by the strict, North American–style grid pattern by which most cities were being built. The Scottish novelist and businessman, John Galt oversaw the planning of Guelph and Goderich, two cities that were designed in a radial plan. Goderich became famous for its octagonal downtown, with cross streets radiating outwards. A courthouse was built in the park in the middle of the octagon. The Huron Road, also built by Galt, connected the cities.

Going Postal

Post offices were the beginnings of many Ontario towns, and postal workers were often the first representatives of the government in new settlements. Because of their influence, the whims of local postmasters led to streets, and even towns, being named by them. For example, the first postmaster to set up shop in the town of Adamsville christened it Acton, after his hometown in northern England. Huntsville's handle is thanks to Miles B. Hunt, its first postmaster. Both Bracebridge and Gravenhurst are named after English towns mentioned in Washington Irving's *Bracebridge Hall*—a novel that a postmaster was reading at the time. The town of Earlton in northern Ontario was named by its first postmaster, Albert Brasher, after his son, George Earl Brasher.

Guelph and Goderich: Not Switched at Birth

A popular myth says that the town plans for Guelph and Goderich were mistakenly switched before construction began. This isn't true; their names were a matter of dispute. The Canada Company, which, with John Galt, oversaw Guelph's development, wanted it named Goderich, after British Prime Minister Viscount Goderich. Galt himself wanted it named Guelph, after the European noble family (also known as the Welfs and the Hanovers) that included Queen Victoria. In the end, Galt won out, and the Canada Company was forced to give the name Goderich to its next project.

Leathertown

Ads encouraging motorists to stop by the "Olde Hide House" in Acton aren't kidding. The town has been dominated by the leather industry since its early beginnings. In 1842, Abraham Nelles established the first tannery. Today, Acton claims the largest leather goods store in the world with 3000 m² of space and 250,000 visitors a year.

OTTAWA

A Capital Idea

It's one of the strange surprises of Canadian politics that a remote logging camp became the national capital. In 1826, Colonel John By oversaw the construction of the Rideau Canal, which connects Kingston to the Ottawa River. It was a military undertaking meant to help transport troops and supplies between Montréal and Lake Ontario in the event that war flared up with the Americans again. (There was a fear that the Americans would try to blockade the St. Lawrence.) The town established at the northern terminus of the canal was named Bytown, after By. Allegedly, By said (somewhat inexplicably) at the time: "This land will be very valuable some day. It will be the capital of this country." During the construction of the canal, the town grew, but its population was almost wiped out by swamp fever. The soldiers stationed in the community abandoned it to escape the epidemic, and the resulting lawlessness led to much violence and crime. In time, though, Bytown became a flourishing logging and mill town.

In 1855, Bytown changed its name to Ottawa, after the Ottawa River, following the trend of towns to adopt aboriginal names. In fact, the word "Ottawa," used by Europeans to describe a nation of people, is actually the Algonquin word *adawe*, meaning "to trade." In 1857, Queen Victoria chose the town as the new capital for Canada—a geographic compromise between the leading contenders, Montréal and Kingston.

Is There a Doctor in the House (of Commons)?
The capital of the United Province of Canada kept moving. The idea was to please everybody, but it also caused problems. When the capital was in Kingston, from 1841 to 1843, there wasn't time to build a parliament building—so the members of parliament met in the local hospital.

The Portable Capital

In 1843, the capital moved to Montréal. Angry Conservatives burned the Parliament Buildings in April 1849, (shouting "no payment for treason!"). They were disturbed by the Rebellion Losses Bill, which they believed might actually benefit some supporters of the rebellion. (The idea behind the bill was to compensate those whose properties were damaged during the rebellions, regardless of their politics.) After that, the capital rotated between Toronto and Québec City, before finally moving Ottawa.

REBELLION, FAST AND BLOODY

A Recipe for Rebellion

Things were boiling over in 1837. Former Toronto mayor William Lyon Mackenzie and his supporters were out of the legislature, and there seemed to be less public support for the extreme radicals. Feeling cornered and desperate, Mackenzie began calling for open rebellion. He gained some support from farmers who had been hard hit by the recent recession. He was also excited by the much bigger and more serious rebellion in Lower Canada and hoped that it would spill over into Upper Canada.

Unlike the French-speaking Lower Canadian *patriotes*, though, who saw their struggle as one for national liberation, Mackenzie's gripe was with the structure of Upper Canada. He was irritated beyond imagination by the top-down government and the unelected elite of the colony, who seemed to him interested mostly in profiting personally from taxation. Mackenzie coined the term "Family Compact" for the tight circle of powerful families that controlled the politics and economy of the colony.

The Upper Canadian rebels also complained about the close, almost theocratic relationship between the government and the Anglican Church (which colonial officials consistently favoured).

On July 31, 1837, Mackenzie issued a Declaration of Independence, laying down principles for an independent republic of Upper Canada—closely based on the American model. Indeed, it seemed possible that Mackenzie might lead Upper Canada to join the United States.

Here Goes Nothing

"Who would live and die a slave?…Come if you dare! Here goes!" wrote Mackenzie a month before the rebellion.

Have a Drink, Get Ready for War

On December 4 and 5, 1837, a few hundred men gathered at Montgomery's Tavern on Yonge Street (near the intersection of Yonge and Lawrence in modern-day North York). The bar was owned by a supporter of Mackenzie's and became a staging point for the main part of the rebellion. John Montgomery did good business that week—but in the end, his support of Mackenzie got his tavern burned down by the militia.

Montgomery's Curse

After the rebellion, Montgomery claimed that he had supported the reform cause, but not Mackenzie's violence. Nevertheless, he received a death sentence, which was later commuted to banishment to the United States. As he was being led away from the court, he said to the judge: "These perjurers…will never die a natural death and when you, sir, and the jury shall have died and perished in hell's flames, John Montgomery will yet be living on Yonge Street." The men who had turned him in to the government and accused him of taking up arms killed themselves. Montgomery returned to Upper Canada in 1843 and rebuilt his tavern. He went on to outlive the judge and all the members of the jury, dying at the ripe old age of 91. Finally, in 1873, the government compensated him $3000 for burning his bar (he claimed it was worth $15,000, plus interest).

The Yonge Street Rising: By the Numbers

Estimates of the number of rebels vary; some people say there were 400, others, 800. In any case, they were poorly disciplined and armed mostly with pikes, farm tools and hunting guns. Mackenzie decided to try for a coup—seizing power while the army was away in Lower Canada, then hoping that the United States would back him.

Death in Toronto

Two men involved in the Yonge Street Rising were hanged. Peter Matthew and Samuel Lount were publicly executed in Toronto, despite Lount's wife pleading directly to the lieutenant-governor to have mercy on him.

An Unhappy Compromise

John Rolph, a prominent English immigrant who supported Mackenzie, suggested an immediate attack while Toronto was vulnerable. Mackenzie's military advisor, Anthony Van Egmond (a veteran Dutch officer and notorious tax cheat who had fought—on both sides—in the Napoleonic Wars), told him the situation was hopeless. He suggested that they withdraw and spend a year training the men, buying more weapons and recruiting a bigger army.

As a compromise, Mackenzie decided to wait a few more days, in the hope that more supporters might show up. The result was the worst of both worlds: no other sympathizers appeared, and by December 7, when they did start marching, the government was prepared. The militia, with two cannons, met the rebels while they marched down Yonge Street and shot at them until they ran back to the tavern. A few hours later, the insurgents were routed, and the rebellion was mostly over. Only one man was killed. The rest were captured or dispersed.

Coat of Many Bullets

Mackenzie intentionally wore several heavy coats during the march and shook out a dozen bullets as he left the battle (he later claimed that, in his life, his unwillingness to die a martyr on Yonge Street was his only cowardly deed). Van Egmond was not so lucky—he was captured, hiding in a barn, and later died in jail.

Provisional "Government"

Mackenzie managed to escape to Navy Island, Canadian territory in the Niagara River. With a small group of his followers, he declared a provisional government of Upper Canada. Unfortunately, when the *Caroline*, his supply ship, was captured by the militia and burned (almost going over Niagara Falls!), Mackenzie was forced to escape to the U.S. He was sent to jail for breaching U.S. neutrality laws—by encouraging Americans to help attack Upper Canada.

The Duncombe Rising

A smaller group of rebels, led by Dr. Charles Duncombe, had massed in the town of Scotland, Ontario, near Brantford. They had planned to march on Hamilton, but gave up and fled when they heard that Mackenzie had been defeated.

Other Skirmishes

A lot of smaller battles—and one not so small—took place in the two years after the 1837 rebellions. Internationally, the romance of Mackenzie's cause seemed to outstrip his actual popularity in Upper Canada. Most of the people who became involved in the subsequent fights were Americans or Europeans.

☛ Detroit River raids: Many small raids occurred in the Detroit River in 1838. A schooner called the *Anne* was seized, and the rebels used it to fire at Fort Malden, south of Windsor. They later ran the ship aground. The same rebels later occupied Fighting Island for a short while.

☛ Invasion of Hickory Island: In February 1838, rebels occupied Hickory Island in the St. Lawrence. "General" Rensselaer van Rensselaer (a lesser-known member of the famous American military and political family, who was not really a general) and "Admiral" Bill Johnston (a notorious St. Lawrence River pirate who, needless to say, was not really an admiral) led the American forces. They planned to land their armies on Hickory Island in the St. Lawrence and then invade the town of Gananoque. From there, they would march on Kingston (Johnston apparently had contacts with pro-rebellion members of the militia, who would sabotage the guns of Fort Henry and open its gates). When the invasion force landed on Hickory Island (with van Rensselaer apparently decked out in a fanciful uniform), however, they got wind that the Canadian militia was prepared to fight them in Gananoque and quickly fled. When the militia inspected Hickory Island afterwards, they found that the rebels had left behind a giant makeshift cannon made out of wood!

☛ Battle of Pelee Island: About 400 rebels landed on Pelee Island—the southernmost inhabited point in Canada—in February 1838. They held it for a few days, before being pushed back across the ice to the American side by the British army and the militia.

☛ Capture of the *Sir Robert Peel*: To get revenge for losing the *Caroline* in May 1838, some rebels seized the Upper Canadian steamer *Sir Robert Peel* in the St. Lawrence and sank it.

☛ Battle of the Short Hills: A small invasion near St. Catharines occurred in June 1838. A few hundred rebels crossed the border, raiding houses and an inn that was sheltering members of the militia. After a quick fight they were pushed back.

☛ Battle of the Windmill: This was the bloodiest battle of the whole rebellion. A group of rebels crossed over the border in November 1838, with a plan to seize Kingston. Nils von Schoultz, a Swedish-Polish soldier of fortune, led the group. The invasion got off to a bad start—the militia cornered the rebels in Prescott, and a few, including von Schoultz, took refuge in a stone windmill. They held out for four days until their ammunition ran out (they even fired off their belt buckles and buttons) and then surrendered. In court, von Schoultz was defended by a 23-year-old lawyer named John Alexander Macdonald—the future prime minister of Canada. Although he lost the case and was sentenced to death, von Schoultz was so impressed with Macdonald's defence that he paid him more than the agreed fee.

☛ Battle of Windsor: The final major action in the rebellion came in December 1838, when 150 men crossed the border at Windsor and killed some militia members before being chased back by the British army.

The Children of Peace: Not So Peaceful

Samuel Lount, one of the two men executed for his part in the rebellion, was a member of a bizarre religious sect, the Children of Peace, that played a major role in Upper Canada.

In 1812, the Children of Peace broke away from a Quaker meeting (or congregation) in Toronto. David Willson, an eccentric, but very charismatic, American immigrant who had only recently joined the Quakers, led the group. Willson took them north, where they founded a colony called Hope, on the site of the modern-day town of Sharon. He saw the struggle of Upper Canadians against the elite circle of the Family Compact as analogous to the struggle of ancient Israelites against the pharaohs. Despite their name, many of the members of the sect took up arms against the government during the rebellion. The sect also rejected the Quakers' opposition to art and music. They formed the first non-military band in Ontario and played and composed music on the first organ in Ontario. Some of their music is still performed today.

The Sharon Temple: Weird and Wonderful

The most famous achievement of the Children of Peace was the construction of the Sharon Temple, one of 19th-century Ontario's most amazing buildings. It was designed in the simple Quaker style, but with diminishing storeys, like a ziggurat. The band sat upstairs, and an opening in the ceiling let the music drift down to the main floor. Willson claimed that the building

was based on the temple of the Israelites, and it had some strange aspects of symbolism, such as the constant use of squares to emphasize square dealing and 12 pillars to represent the 12 apostles.

The group never numbered more than 500 at one time and quickly fell apart after Willson's death in 1866.

PLAN B

Durham's Report

All the fighting of 1837 led Britain to appoint John Lambton (First Earl of Durham and better known as Lord Durham) to write a report. Durham was also nicknamed "Radical Jack" for his liberal politics—though his view of French Canadians was far from liberal. Durham visited Canada in 1838, spending almost all his time in Lower Canada. In the end, he recommended a fully elected government, an end to the controversial clergy reserves and judicial reform.

A Man With a (Questionable) Plan

Durham also suggested that Upper and Lower Canada be merged into a single colony, where francophones could be (according to Durham) outvoted and ultimately assimilated. Durham is fondly remembered in Ontario as the father of democracy, but he is still hated by many in Québec for his policy of assimilation. By 1841, Upper and Lower Canada were joined into the United Province of Canada.

The Rebellion's Legacy

It's hard to say how much the Upper Canada rebellion accomplished. Its supporters quickly claimed responsibility for Durham's reforms—but the report was written while fighting was still going on in Upper Canada. Durham wasn't sent to North America because of the minor skirmishes in Upper Canada—he came because the British government feared an all-out revolution in Lower Canada. In the end, there's not much that can be specifically credited to the rebellion, though life did get better in Upper Canada.

Canada West:
The First, Best West
(1841–1867)

With the stroke of a pen, Upper Canada was transformed into Canada West, one half of the United Province of Canada. Suddenly, Upper Canadian leaders had to learn to work with their French-speaking counterparts from Lower Canada.

The results were some of the most extraordinary compromises, not to mention a dust-up or two. At home, things remained dicey. Canada West's streets turned into sectarian battlegrounds. And then the Fenians came over the hills...

POLITICS IN PARLIAMENT

Distinct Societies

One of the rules imposed by the Union Act, which united Upper and Lower Canada (or Canada West and Canada East, as they would now be called), was that each side would get equal representation in Parliament. This was despite the fact that Canada East had 650,000 citizens, compared to 450,000 in Canada West—a detail that upset many people in Canada East. They demanded representation by population, at least until the population of Canada West grew bigger than Canada East—at which point, their positions switched.

There was duplication in government as well—two attorneys general, for instance, represented each half of the province. Canada East kept French civil law, while Canada West used English law. The two colonies made an odd pair. During the previous 50 years, they had grown very different from one another. The result was a permanently divided Parliament—not unlike federal politics today.

Nitty Gritty Politics

The first real political parties in Canada started to appear in the decades before Confederation. With more power in the hands of elected officials, rather than the Family Compact, the Reformers turned into a formal party.

The more radical Reformers, upset that change was happening too slowly, got the nickname "Clear Grits" from their supporters. Party member David Christie coined the term, calling the radicals "all sand and no dirt; clear grit all the way through"—a reference to the ideal mix for masonry. It also suggested that they were straightforward and had "true grit," or fortitude. Mackenzie himself was pardoned and allowed back to

Toronto—where he quickly joined the Clear Grits and went back to his radical reform agenda, albeit without starting any more rebellions.

In 1857, the Reformers and Clear Grits were reunited. To this day, the Liberal Party—which the Reformers became after Confederation—is nicknamed the "Grits."

On the other hand (the right hand, that is), the opponents of the Reformers—no longer able to rule through unelected means, began to organize their own party. The group, based around William Henry Draper—a Toronto lawyer nicknamed "Sweet William" because of his smooth, polished style—became the Tories, and later, the Conservatives.

When Outlaws Make Law

Incidentally, the term "Tory" goes back centuries earlier to Britain. It started as an insult aimed at the conservative bloc of politicians by their opponents, meaning "Irish outlaw."

DID YOU KNOW?

Reform politician Robert Baldwin was a morbid, and down-right weird, guy. His wife died during childbirth after a failed Caesarean section. Baldwin blamed himself for her death and spiralled into a deep depression that lasted most of his life. When he died 10 years later, his will instructed that his coffin be chained to his wife's and that their love letters be placed in each other's coffins. Finally, Baldwin wrote that he wanted an incision in his body that imitated the Caesarean section that killed his wife. Baldwin's daughter went along with the first two requests, but wouldn't comply with the third. But his son felt guilty, and a few days after his father's burial, had him dug up and the incision made.

THE WILD WEST

The Irish Problem

With mass Irish immigration—both Catholic and Protestant—
to North America, came complicated and violent Irish politics.
Militant factions quickly established themselves in Canada West.

Orange You Glad You're in the Order?
On one side was the Orange Order—a fraternal Protestant
group that supported the British occupation of Ireland. With
connections made to the old Protestant elite of the Family
Compact—some of them Irish themselves—the Order quickly
came to control the police forces of Canada West. It exerted
huge influence in politics, too—in many towns, it was considered unthinkable to be elected as a politician or appointed as
a judge without membership in the Order.

The Fenians

On the other side was the Fenian Brotherhood—a militant
group of Irish Catholics that was committed to winning Irish
independence from Britain. They had a lot more power and
influence in the United States, especially in cities such as New
York and Boston—though they set up chapters in most Ontario
communities, too.

"And we'll go and capture Canada, for we've nothing else to do." These are the words to a Fenian marching song. Why isn't Canada called "New Ireland" today? Well, possibly because the Fenians were a little over-optimistic in their goals. Today, Ontarians remember the Fenians mostly because of the Fenian Raids—a series of border attacks that happened in the 1860s. Many Fenians had joined the U.S. army during the American Civil War in order to get the military training they thought they needed for an upcoming Irish war of independence. As the Civil War ended and not much seemed to be happening in Ireland, they got the idea to invade Canada. They hoped—with forces of a few hundred men—to capture the country, rename it New Ireland and ransom it back to Britain for old Ireland.

In 1866, a group of 500 armed Fenians crossed the Niagara River and headed for Hamilton and Toronto. The local militia caught up with them, only to be overwhelmed by the Fenians in the bloody Battle of Ridgeway. After the siege—which seems to have confused everyone—both sides retreated. The Fenians ran into another military force that had landed at Fort Erie, and defeated them, too. More Fenians were waiting on the American side but weren't able to cross because the U.S. navy had posted a ship upriver to keep them back. With massive numbers of army units moving in from Hamilton and Toronto, the invading Fenians decided to go back across the border and surrender.

The Fenian raids seemed to make the Canadian public even keener on Confederation. A unified, independent country seemed like it would be better organized and prepared for future threats. Plus, the British-hating Fenians would have less reason to attack it. The armoury system—with tiny military bases in many towns—was developed to deal with any intimidation from groups such as the Fenians.

McGee Assassination

Thomas D'Arcy McGee, Father of Confederation, was believed to have been gunned down by a Fenian in 1868. McGee was an immigrant who had once been a militant Irish nationalist, but later denounced the Fenians' violent tactics. McGee is one of only two Canadian politicians to be assassinated (the other was the Québec Labour Minister Pierre Laporte, strangled by FLQ members in 1970).

Forty suspects were rounded up after McGee's death, including Sir John A. Macdonald's chauffeur. Patrick J. Wheelan, a local tailor, who was found with a loaded gun in his pocket, was convicted of the murder and hanged. It was the last public hanging in Canada. Wheelan was never proven to be a member of the Fenians, and to this day, many believe he was innocent. Just before he was hanged, he claimed that he knew the actual murderer but would not give his name.

In 2005, the Museum of Civilization in Gatineau bought Wheelan's gun for $150,000. In the same year, Library and Archives Canada reported that the fatal bullet had gone missing from its storage within the previous five years.

Wheelan's ghost is said to haunt the old Ottawa prison, now a youth hostel. It's said that he can still be heard murmuring the Lord's Prayer, his last words.

DID YOU KNOW?

The author Charles Dickens visited Toronto during a book tour in 1841. While he liked the city, Dickens wrote that he was disgusted by the "rabid Toryism" of Toronto and the violence of the Orangemen.

Orange Riots

Despite its political influence, the Orange Order wasn't above stirring up violence in the streets when things weren't going its way. This was particularly dangerous when police, mostly Orangemen themselves, wouldn't arrest or control rioters who were members of the fraternity, or when firemen, also members, took to lighting fires rather than putting them out. In fact, it was said that the many informal and sectarian volunteer fire departments in Toronto started more fires than they doused.

On June 29, 1855, two rival groups of volunteer firemen responded to a call and wound up fighting each other instead. When the police showed up to break up the riot, both groups of firemen turned on them. Several firemen were arrested. Later, the police constables deliberately botched their testimony in court so as to let their fellow Orangemen off the hook.

On July 13, 1865, a group of Toronto volunteer firemen, who were in the Orange Order, began brawling with a troupe of travelling clowns that they'd come across in a brothel. So began the Circus Riots, some of the wildest violence the city had seen. The clowns won the brawl, but the next day mobs of firemen attacked the circus and burned it down. The police refused to intervene, and order wasn't restored until the mayor called in the army. When the firemen were hauled into court, police refused to testify to seeing them at the skirmish.

Rival Marches

Nothing caused more violence on a regular basis than the annual St. Patrick's Day parade, put on by Catholics, and the Orangemen's Parade, put on by Protestants. A man was stabbed to death by Orangemen in the 1858 Toronto parade, but the police chief, who was present, refused to testify against the murderer. The Orange Order parades—commemorating the victory of the Protestant King William of Orange over Irish Catholics in the Battle of the Boyne in 1690—would deliberately go through Catholic neighbourhoods. It was traditional for brick-throwing Catholics to try to knock "King Billy" off his horse as he passed by.

GET OUTTA TOWN!

The Railway Boom

In the 1850s, Canada West was nailing down railway tracks as fast as it could. In 1855, the Northern Railway linked Toronto to Collingwood on Georgian Bay—a huge shortcut for Great Lakes shipping. In the same year, the Great Western Railway connected Niagara Falls to Windsor through Hamilton, and continued from Hamilton to Toronto. In 1859, the massive Grand Trunk Railway linked Toronto and Montréal. The railways turned Canada West (and East) upside down. Suddenly, people could travel across the province in a matter of hours.

Railways Build Cities

The railway enabled commercial goods—especially timber—to get quickly to the American market, and likewise, local stores were flooded with goods from the U.S. Suddenly, there was more demand for industry to produce competing products— and the industrial revolution really began in Canada West. With the American Civil War raging throughout the 1860s, the U.S. economy was swamped, and Canadians got rich exporting goods and crops south. The whole landscape changed, with new tracks, bridges, stations and roundhouses turning up everywhere. Toronto saw huge growth, and industrial cities such as Hamilton, London and Stratford developed economies completely based around the railway.

In 1853, the first train engine built in Canada West was completed at James Good's Locomotive Works. It was named the *Toronto*.

Disaster Strikes

Railways were safe, but they were far from perfect. Between September 1853 and October 1854, no less than 79 people were killed and 70 injured in 17 separate accidents on the Great Western Railway. In 1857, a passenger train derailed on a bridge and plunged through the ice of the Desjardins Canal below, killing 70 people—the first truly major rail disaster in the province.

Suspend Your Disbelief

Imagine crossing over Niagara Falls in a train weighing hundreds of tonnes or more—on a suspension bridge! In 1855, such a bridge provided the first rail link across the Niagara River (it replaced an earlier crossing, built in 1848, that could not handle rail). Eventually, in 1897, it too was replaced by the steel arch of the Whirlpool Rapids Bridge.

An Air Line that Stayed Grounded

Ontario had its first airline in 1871—despite the fact that airplanes weren't invented until 1903. In railway terms, an "air line" (spelled as two words) is a long, straight stretch of track that gives a smooth, fast trip. The Great Western Railway's Canada Air Line ran over 230 kilometres from Glencoe to Fort Erie.

ROAMING PIGS AND OTHER ASPECTS OF LIFE IN CANADA WEST

Off the Pigs

Livestock running wild was a major problem in 19th-century Ontario. In 1849, the town of Niagara (now Niagara Falls) put out a proclamation—simply titled "Swine"—describing "great inconvenience or damage...experienced by the Public from Swine running at large within the limits of the town of Niagara." It threatened to impound all free-roaming pigs and charge their owners fines.

Until the mid 20th century, many urban Ontarians, even in downtown Toronto, kept livestock in their houses and yards. It was not unusual to see chicken- and goat-breeding operations running out of homes in Toronto's poorer neighbourhoods. Naturally, horses were common sights, too. The city of Toronto maintained public horse-watering troughs at most major intersections up until the 1940s.

Universities

The 1840s and 1850s were times of growth for universities in Canada West. All of them started off as religious, though most became secular in time. Some were amalgamated over the next decades into the University of Toronto. The university's college system allowed it to combine different institutions with different cultures and purposes.

Ontario Universities Started in the 19th Century

Name	Denomination	Year Founded	Currently Part of
King's College	Anglican (though by the time it opened, it was secular)	1827 (though classes didn't start until 1853)	University of Toronto
The Upper Canada Academy (later Victoria College)	Methodist	1837	University of Toronto
Queen's University	Presbyterian	1841	Queen's University
College of Bytown	Catholic	1848	University of Ottawa
Trinity College	Anglican	1852	University of Toronto
St. Michael's College	Catholic	1852	University of Toronto
The Western University	Anglican	1878	University of Western Ontario
McMaster University	Baptist	1887	McMaster University

DID YOU KNOW?

Toronto's infamous Don Jail—also one of its oldest surviving public buildings—was built in 1865. Nearly 100 years later, in 1962, it was the site of Canada's last executions. On December 11 of that year, Ronald Turpin and Arthur Lucas were hanged after being convicted of murder.

Irish Immigration

In the 1840s, substantial numbers of poor Irish immigrants began arriving in Canada (of 90,000 immigrants to Canada in 1847, 70,000 were Irish). Disease was widespread among them. Many died in quarantine on Grosse Île, the massive containment station for immigrants in the St. Lawrence, near Québec City. Others died in the holding buildings, or "fever sheds," of Kingston and Toronto. Toronto's first Catholic bishop, Michael Power, died of typhus while tending to sick Irish immigrants in 1847.

DID YOU KNOW?

Alexander Robert Dunn of Toronto was the first Canadian to win the Commonwealth's most prestigious military award, the Victoria Cross. He fought with the British army in the Battle of Balaclava in 1854 during the Crimean War. So far, 94 Canadians have been awarded the Victoria Cross. The last was Robert Hampton Gray of Trail, BC, after his death in Japan on August 9, 1945. He was also the last Canadian to die in World War II.

Agincourt

John Hill founded the community of Agincourt, now a part of Toronto, in 1858. It got its unusual name because Canada East politician Louis-Hippolyte Lafontaine promised to help secure funding for Hill only if he gave the new settlement a French name. Slyly, Hill chose the name of a town in northern France—featured in Shakespeare's *Henry V*—where England scored its biggest victory over France in the Hundred Years' War.

All That Glitters Is Gold

The town of Eldorado sprang up around the site of Canada's first gold rush. Decades before enthusiasts of the get-rich-quick way of life headed for the Yukon, they were digging in Canada West. One legend says that a fisherman first discovered the gold. His companion, who had been sitting next to him by the side of the river, got up and left because the mosquitoes had become too much of a nuisance. The fisherman looked over and saw that the man had been sitting on a huge mound of gold. Another legend says that a horse, kicking at the ground, revealed the gold. Indeed, most of the Eldorado gold was close to the surface. Once digging began, it was quickly exhausted.

Oil's Well that Begins Well

North America's first oil well—and one of the first in the world—was dug at Oil Springs, Canada West, in 1858. The use of oil had only just been expanded beyond lamps, and its discovery sparked a mini-boom in western Ontario. Oil City and Petrolia sprung up. Petrolia, which now calls itself "Canada's Victorian Oil Town," was the centre of the boom. Its first residents, known as "hard oilers," became the world's first oil experts, and they travelled the world to find work in a total of 87 countries. Petrolians have ended up in Alberta, Saudi Arabia, Texas, Russia and elsewhere. Back in Petrolia's oil museum, the Petrolia Discovery, oil is still being pumped out today, albeit very slowly.

Salt of the Earth

In 1865, oil prospectors drilling near Goderich hit on a much older commodity—salt. They discovered Canada's largest deposit of rock salt—stretching deep out underneath Lake Huron. The massive salt mines and shipping port that were constructed became the cornerstone of Goderich's economy.

DID YOU  KNOW?

Emily Stowe of Norwich, Ontario, became Canada's first female doctor after graduating from New York's Medical College for Women in 1867 (at the time, no medical schools in Canada would take women). But she did not get around to applying for a licence to practise in Ontario until 1880. Stowe was prompted to study medicine after her husband—also a doctor—died of tuberculosis. Augusta Stowe—Emily's daughter—became the first women to graduate from medical school in Canada in 1883. The first practising female doctor in Canada was Stratford's Jenny Kidd Trout, who graduated from Women's Medical College in Pennsylvania in 1875 and was licensed in the same year.

NATIONAL ASPIRATIONS

Old Macdonald

In 1857, a Scottish lawyer living in Kingston, with a penchant for alcohol and extreme shrewdness, became co-leader of the United Province. Sir John A. Macdonald, with the help of his Canada East counterpart, Georges-Étienne Cartier, became one of Ontario's most successful (and—for his role in the Louis Riel affair—most controversial) politicians. He resigned his leadership in 1858 but was back in power fast—through clever legal loopholes—in a manoeuvre that was called the "Double Shuffle." Macdonald got around the rule that forced ministers in a government to step down (and stand for re-election) when they were defeated in a confidence motion. He simply appointed everyone, including himself, to different positions than those that they originally held—and then switched them back to their old positions the next day.

Two Birthdays are Better Than One
Recently, some people have suggested making Macdonald's birthday a national holiday—but what was his birthday? Apparently, he was born around midnight. It was officially recorded as January 10, 1815, but Macdonald himself celebrated it on January 11.

All in the Family

Macdonald—Sir John, that is—was not the only politician in his family.

His son, Hugh John Macdonald, went on to become premier of Manitoba. Like his father, Hugh was a Conservative and an opponent of Louis Riel. He actually participated in fighting against the Métis during the battles of the Riel Rebellion. Later, Hugh was put in charge of banishing strikers to labour camps after the Winnipeg General Strike.

John Sanfield Macdonald—a distant cousin of Sir John—became the first premier of Ontario. John S. Macdonald is not well remembered by Ontarians today, even though his statue stands outside the provincial legislature. He led a Liberal-Conservative coalition government and was the last Catholic premier for 132 years—until Premier Dalton McGuinty. John S. and John A. often collaborated in politics—it was said they "hunted in pairs," though they also sometimes conspired against each other. John S. was often criticized for his informal style of governing, budgeting money in non-specific estimates and openly appointing his friends to important roles.

Considering Confederation
Confederation was popular in Canada West for lots of reasons. People were upset with the single government that ruled the United Province of Canada. They wanted more local powers for the English-speaking half of the province, like Upper Canada

had had in the old days. Big business wanted room to expand and closely eyed the East Coast, and even the Prairies, as potential resource colonies.

By 1867, Confederation was a fact. The old United Canada government, now based in Ottawa, morphed into the Canadian federal government. Some of its powers were given to the new provinces. Canada West had to change its name to avoid confusion with Canada, the country. The name Ontario was chosen. A new country with four provinces—Ontario, Québec, New Brunswick and Nova Scotia—was created.

Dominion of Canada, 1867

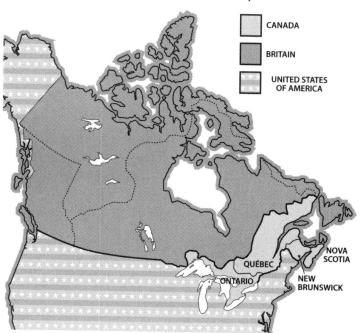

CANADA

BRITAIN

UNITED STATES OF AMERICA

From "Beautiful Lake" to a Beautiful Province?

The name "Ontario" is probably a corruption of one of three similar Wendat words: *onitariio*, meaning "beautiful lake"; *kanadario*, meaning "beautiful water"; and *skanadario*, meaning "very pretty lake." It is not clear how accurate any of these translations are, since there are no longer any Wendat speakers today. All of the translations go back to early French missionaries. Linguists say that Iroquoian place names never used descriptions like "beautiful," so it's possible that the words simply mean "body of water." The name originally applied to Lake Ontario, but European settlers gradually applied it to even bigger areas along the shore.

The Maple Leaf Forever

Toronto's Alexander Muir wrote Canada's alternate national anthem, "The Maple Leaf Forever," in 1867. Muir, a bit of a fanatical patriot and an Orangeman who had fought on the Canadian side of the Fenian raid at Niagara, said he was inspired to write the lyrics when he saw leaves falling from a maple tree. Generations of Ontario schoolchildren sang "The Maple Leaf Forever," along with "O Canada" by Québec's Calixa Lavallée, but it eventually became unpopular because of its pro-British lyrics. French Canadians always felt that the song was offensive, and its chorus of "the thistle, shamrock, rose entwined, the maple leaf forever!" seem to leave out Canadians of non-British ancestry.

Ontario, Canada: Into the Heart of a New Country (1867–1914)

Once again, with the stroke of a pen, Ontario was tossed into a new world. It was now the most populous province in the heart of a country that would soon span from the Atlantic to the Pacific and the Arctic Oceans.

Industrialization and capitalism were quickly bringing an end to the quaint, British ways of the old elite. Towards the end of the 19th century, the first major waves of non-British or German immigration began, bringing whole neighbourhoods of newcomers from southern and eastern Europe. A northern expanse, mysterious—and profitable—was added to the province and quickly developed. Those who could afford it bought some of the exciting new inventions that were coming out—such as bicycles, cars and airplanes. Those who couldn't sometimes found themselves stuck in the huge slums of Toronto.

NORTHERN ONTARIO:
A DREAM AND A NIGHTMARE

Algonquin Park

In 1893, Algonquin Provincial Park—the first provincial park in Ontario—was born. Most of its area had already been devastated by clear-cutting, and there was growing public concern in the province that no natural space would be left for preservation or recreation. It was originally intended as a national park, but the provincial government seemed keener to fund it than the federal government. As the forests began to grow back, Algonquin became a major tourist destination. In 1897, a railway line was built through the park, transporting both visitors and logs, and the park continued to be serviced by rail until 1959. In 1902, the first group of artists arrived at Canoe Lake, establishing Algonquin as a mecca for wilderness painting and paving the way for the Group of Seven.

Group of Seven? Or 10? Or 11?

The Group of Seven actually had 10 members. In 1920, the first seven were: Franklin Carmichael, Lawren Harris, A.Y. Jackson, Frank Johnston, Arthur Lismer, J.E.H. MacDonald and Frederick Varley. Frank Johnston left the group in 1926. Three new members joined in 1926, 1931 and 1932 respectively: A.J. Casson, LeMoine Fitzgerald and Edwin Holgate. The most famous artist to be associated with the Group—Tom Thomson—was never a member. He died before it was founded.

The artists made their names by applying impressionistic techniques to landscapes of Ontario's rugged north. They worked out of a studio that still stands on Severn Street in Toronto. In 1933, they disbanded, but soon after reformed as the Canadian Group of Painters. The last surviving member of the group was A.J. Casson, who died in 1992.

DID YOU KNOW?

Tom Thomson died in a mysterious incident in 1917. The skilled canoeist was discovered dead after a trip across the calm waters of Algonquin Park's Canoe Lake. He was found with his temple badly bruised and with a copper fishing line wrapped around his ankle. The cause of his death—officially called a canoeing accident—was never fully explained. Many of his friends believed that he had been murdered after a dispute over money with a local lodge owner. This theory says that the fishing wire was originally attached to weights, designed to make his body sink to the bottom of the lake. Those who believe his death was an accident think he probably died after he stood up in the canoe to urinate, then tripped and hit his head on the gunwale.

Thomson was quickly buried near the lake, but his family had him reburied in his hometown of Leith, near Owen Sound. Some people believed that his body was never actually moved— and Thomson's girlfriend continued to tend a gravesite at Canoe Lake. Amateur historian Judge William Little became fascinated with the case and wrote a book in which he claimed to have dug up the grave at Canoe Lake in 1956 and discovered Thomson's remains. But his assertions were later discredited when scientific testing proved the remains were not Thomson's.

Cottage Country Begins

An even bigger name than Algonquin, when it comes to city-dwellers wanting to escape into nature, is Muskoka. Today, Muskoka County, due north of Toronto, is among the most coveted real estate in Canada, with massive cottages outstripping many houses in Toronto, both in size and price. (Never call Muskoka "the Muskokas" around locals. They will remind you, hotly, that there is only one Muskoka. The habit of pluralizing the name is probably copied from the Hamptons, the refuge of New York City's elite.)

Arguably, Muskoka's first cottagers were James Bain and John Campbell. At a time when everyone who could afford it travelled south or to Europe for holidays, the wealthy friends made the unusual decision to holiday in the north. At the time, no roads or railways went north of Barrie, so they had to proceed by boat. When they reached Gravenhurst (or the future site of Gravenhurst), they found that the locals in the rough logging country had never heard of tourists. They took the men to be land surveyors or travelling preachers. Bain and Campbell later teamed up with other adventurous young men to form the Muskoka Club, which organized hiking and canoeing trips in the county. They bought an island in Lake Joseph, which they gave the exotic name "Yoho Cucaba" (actually a shortening of the names of the club's members: Young, Howland, Cummings, Campbell and Bain).

Muskoka's first upscale hotel was built in 1870 on Lake Rosseau. Its first cottage was built in 1875 by James "the Chief" Campbell (the father of Muskoka Club co-founder, John Campbell, who liked the scenery but was less interested in camping than was his son). The location of the cottage became known as Chief's Island.

Lumberjack's Waltz

Lumberjacks—strong young men crowded into camps far away from home—were notorious for their extracurricular activities. They often fought each other in bloody fights. In the late 19th century camps of northern Ontario, some "rules" developed for the "sport." It would start with each man hurling a big stone onto the ground, like a gauntlet, to demonstrate his strength. Then the men proceeded to wrestle until one was too badly injured to get up. The winner then marked the loser for life by stomping on or kicking his face with his spiked boots. After recovery (or if they recovered), losing men would usually sport beards to cover the scars.

Boarding House Reach

Another sport associated with logging camps was "reaching." At suppertime, the men would gather, and food would simply be thrown onto the table. Those who grabbed the fastest got to eat the most. The phrase "having a boarding-house reach," meaning having quick reflexes, exists to this day.

Eagle's Nest

Overlooking the town of Bancroft is a cliff known as the Eagle's Nest. The hill is known for its view and its huge, 15-metre-long icicles in the winter.

Originally, it was home to eagles—as its name suggests—but early settlers, afraid of the birds, killed them. In 1918, a local youth shot a huge eagle that had a wingspan of 2 metres.

In 1883, a local couple actually reported an eagle attempting to make off with their baby, who had been playing behind the house. It only gave up the child after being attacked with a broom and a rake.

Billa Flint

The town of Bancroft got its name thanks to crusty Senator Billa Flint, a fanatical supporter of temperance who boasted that he had had only six weeks of education before starting to work at age 11. He went on to become a wealthy land speculator and businessman, military officer, philanthropist and politician. In 1879, he renamed York Mills after his mother-in-law, Elizabeth Ann Bancroft. Flint also founded the mill towns of Troy (now Actinolite) and Flint's Mills (now Flinton).

Art, Bill... Can't We All Get Along?

In 1867, the federal government began construction on the Dawson Road, connecting Lake Superior to Manitoba. The Wolsley expedition, travelling the route on its way to put down the Riel Rebellion, named its supply depot Prince Arthur's Landing. Prince Arthur himself—the son of Queen Victoria— only "landed" in town in 1890. Later, the Canadian Pacific Railway decided to shorten Prince Arthur's Landing to Port Arthur.

A battle started up—lasting many years—between Port Arthur and its neighbour, the old fur-trading town of Fort William, for control of the Great Lakes shipping. Both vied to be the main port to which grain would be shipped from the West and continue down into southern Ontario. The first grain elevator in Canada, west of the Great Lakes, was built in Port Arthur in 1883. In 1970, Fort William and Port Arthur finally buried the hatchet and merged to become Thunder Bay.

Little Ontario Grows

Ontario was a newborn province in a newborn country in 1867. It had appropriately teeny proportions—only about one-eighth of its current size. Ontario started as the area south of Lake Nipissing. The massive north of the province, very sparsely populated, was added on in stages, and it didn't come without a fight.

In the mid 19th century, the Hudson's Bay Company still controlled the north, but the fur trade was dying, and the demand for lumber and minerals was rising. Ontario beat out Manitoba (and the possibility of forming a new province in the north) and managed to expand upwards.

This was one fight that Sir John A. Macdonald lost to the Ontario Liberal government of Oliver Mowat. Macdonald was promoting a bigger Manitoba that included the Rainy River and Lake of the Woods area. He moved Manitoba's border east—despite the fact that an arbitration panel had ruled in Ontario's favour. The fight became so heated in the contested territory that both sides sent police to the area (who promptly arrested each other). Eventually, Mowat won by going over Macdonald's head to the Privy Council in England, which ruled in Ontario's favour. Mowat returned triumphant to Toronto and 100,000 people gathered to cheer his arrival.

In 1889, the British Parliament voted to uphold Ontario's right to everything south of the English and Albany Rivers—including today's cities of Sudbury, Thunder Bay, Sault Ste. Marie and Timmins. The northernmost area—going up past the Albany River and stretching far around Hudson's Bay, was added in 1912.

There's a New Ontario

The northern territory incorporated into the province was originally nicknamed "New Ontario" (and the south was labelled, appropriately, "Old Ontario"). As time went by and the north became less "new," the name faded. In French, northern Ontario is still commonly called *Nouvel Ontario* (similar to the north of Québec, added around the same time, which is known as *Nouveau Québec*).

Multicultural North

Unlike most of northern Canada, northern Ontario was multicultural from the beginning. When it joined the province, an industrial boom began, drawing immigrants from all over, adding to the Cree and Ojibwa communities and those of early Anglo settlers. Northern Ontario became particularly popular with people from Finland and Italy. In fact, there are still large Finnish and Italian communities in Sault Ste. Marie, Thunder Bay and Sudbury. Large numbers of French Canadians moved from southern Québec, making half (or more than half) of the populations of many northern communities French-speaking today.

Silver Eyes

According to legend, a silver-mining rush began in 1903 when local blacksmith Fred La Rose threw his hammer at what he thought were the gleaming eyes of a fox peering at him from behind a rock. It turned out to be a vein of pure silver. By 1908, a bustling town of 7000, named Cobalt, had sprung up on the spot. It had 18 hotels, four banks, six churches and a multicultural population of English, French and Eastern European settlers. Between 1903 and 1920, when the rush ended, $264 million worth of silver was shipped out of Cobalt.

Green Eyes

Ontario grew rich in the late 19th century, but its wealth was based on exploiting the north. Rather than selling the land, the provincial government charged exorbitant rents and fees to logging and timber companies. This kept taxes low in southern Ontario and kept most people happy. Premier Mowat openly admitted this strategy, and the provincial government totalled surpluses of $17 million between 1872 and 1896—an enormous amount for that day.

WORKING FOR A LIVING?

Women at Work

While logging was the biggest employer overall in Ontario, garment factories were the most significant industry in Toronto. About three-quarters of garment workers were women, and most were recent immigrants. "I don't treat the men bad, but I even it up by taking advantage of the women," boasted one factory boss. Women were paid, on average, half of what men received.

Typographers' Strike

Sir John A. Macdonald—too shrewd to miss an opportunity to tweak his rival George Brown's nose—poked his head into the politics of labour unions, too. Surprisingly, Macdonald formed an alliance with striking Toronto typographers in 1872. They teamed up to defeat Brown, an old Liberal party enemy of Macdonald, who had personal reasons to oppose the strike. He was the owner of the *Globe*, and he employed many of the typographers. The Trades Union Act, which allowed for collective bargaining, was the beginning of a powerful labour movement in Canada.

The First Labour Day

The world's first celebration of Labour Day happened on April 15, 1872, in Toronto, and featured marching bands and parading union members. Ten years later, in 1882, the tradition of celebrating an annual Labour Day was started. Visiting American union members were so impressed that they copied the idea.

After the birth of Labour Day's more militant cousin—May Day—in Chicago in 1886, politicians were glad to promote a gentler holiday for unions. On June 28, 1894, Labour Day became an official holiday in the U.S., and on July 23 of the same year, it was declared an official holiday in Canada.

THE BUSINESS OF BUSINESS

Eaton's

In 1869, Irish immigrant Timothy Eaton opened the first Eaton's store in St. Mary's, but it was his second location in Toronto that proved to be a huge money-maker. Soon Eaton's expanded its scope to a new concern—the catalogue order business. Within 25 years of its founding, it was already calling itself "Canada's greatest store." In 1977, it launched downtown Toronto's biggest shopping mall, the Eaton's Centre; however, the chain went bankrupt in 1999, and the American department store Sears bought its remains.

DID YOU KNOW?

A giant statue of Timothy Eaton was bought by the Royal Ontario Museum after the chain's collapse. It is considered good luck for business people to rub Timothy's toe. The massive Timothy Eaton Memorial Church in Toronto, largely paid for by its namesake, stands as a reminder of Eaton's philanthropy.

Bay Street Slumming

Today, Toronto's Bay Street is known as Canada's centre of wealth and corporate headquarters, but in the 19th century, it was considered a slum, lined with workers' tenements, shacks and garment factories.

Santa Claus Parade

Eaton's Santa Claus Parade started in Toronto in 1905 and later expanded to Winnipeg and Montréal. The parade event continues today and remains among the biggest events in Toronto. The Macy's Thanksgiving Parade in New York City was modelled after the Eaton's Santa Claus Parade.

Massey-Harris

One of the most powerful companies in Ontario was formed in 1890, when Hart Massey and Alanson Harris merged their farm implement factories. For years, Massey-Harris (later Massey-Ferguson) was a giant in the farm machinery industry, and it made the Massey family rich and powerful. The Masseys founded Massey Hall and Massey College, and Vincent Massey became the first Canadian-born governor general. His brother, Raymond, went on to become a successful stage actor and Hollywood star. (He got his start in Siberia, of all places, organizing a show for the Canadian army during its ill-fated invasion of Russia in 1919.)

Niagara Falls

You think Niagara Falls is commercialized today? In the mid to late 19th century, all the land along the shore of the Niagara River, facing the Falls, was privately owned. Tourists had to pay landowners for a chance to peek at them (the Falls!), through holes in (strategically placed) fences. Public criticism of this system led to the government buying up most of the land and turning it into parks.

The Lure of the Falls

The tourism industry at Niagara Falls—the most popular holiday destination in Canada—continued to grow. It was spurred on by the work of daredevils attracted to the Falls. French acrobat, Jean François Gravelet (better known by his stage name "Blondin"), was the first person to cross the Niagara Gorge by tightrope in 1859. He actually did it 17 times, one time stopping in the middle to cook and eat an omelette on a portable stove; other times carrying his manager on his back, wearing a blindfold or walking on stilts. In 1829, Sam Patch, an American stunt-performer, was the first known person to go over the Falls and survive. In 1901, American schoolteacher Annie Edson Taylor was the first person to do it in a barrel.

First Car

The first car maker in Ontario was Robert McLaughlin— though McLaughlin himself hated cars (he considered them noisy, smelly, dangerous and a "passing fad"). By the time he launched his first car, the Irish immigrant had already made his fortune in manufacturing. A small home business building axe handles eventually became the huge McLaughlin Carriage Company, based in Oshawa. His sons convinced him to strike a deal with an American company, Buick, to make "McLaughlin" cars with Buick motors.

In 1908, 154 McLaughlins rolled off the assembly line. In 1918, General Motors (a merger between Buick and Chevrolet) bought out the company, and General Motors Canada was established—with Sam McLaughlin, son of Robert, as its president. He kept a firm grip on the company and only retired as chairman of the board in 1967 at age 96.

Since his first ride in 1904, Sam McLaughlin had been a huge car enthusiast. (Before that he had been a bicycle fanatic, once riding all the way from Oshawa to Brockville and back on a penny farthing–style bike, known for its huge front wheel.)

Ford built its first Ontario plant in 1904, and after World War I, car ownership exploded. In 1914, horse carriage traffic made up over half of road activity in the London area; but by 1922, it was down to three percent. By the 1920s, automobile manufacturing was the biggest industry in Ontario, as it remains today.

LIFE IN VICTORIAN AND EDWARDIAN ONTARIO

Yum

In 1882, the *Globe* called Toronto's water "drinkable sewage."

Fructing Around

Here's a word to test your vocabulary: usufructuary. In 1888, in a landmark case, the Privy Council ruled that First Nations' right to the land was "usufructuary," meaning that they were restricted in their right to occupy it, build on it or keep others off it. Victor Savino, a contemporary First Nations land claims lawyer gave the word a different definition: "Indians were used and fructed."

First or Worst?

Canada First was a small but influential group. It pushed for Canadian nationalism and the development of a distinct and unified Canadian identity. Between 1874 and 1876, it ran the *Nation*, a newspaper expressing these ideas. The National Club, a meeting place founded by the group, still exists today, and most nationalist cultural projects in Canada sprang out of Canada First. Critics said Canada First was really more about trying to make the rest of Canada more like Ontario (or like an idealized version of Ontario): white, Protestant and British.

Canada Firsters were an eccentric (and often racist) bunch. Charles Mair, a poet who had volunteered to fight against Louis Riel, wrote a five-act Shakespearian-style play about the War of 1812 (with the Americans as the fools and villains). Another group member, Robert Haliburton claimed, inexplicably, that

Canadians were the New World's Norsemen, possessing their mystical, racially superior qualities. Goldwin Smith, a University of Toronto professor (who helped found the Art Gallery of Ontario) and one of the group's first members, eventually left and began publishing pamphlets urging Canada to join the United States.

In addition to launching the first writing contests and poetry readings in Canada, the group was responsible for whipping up anti-French and anti-Métis feelings in Ontario, which led to the Red River Rebellion being quickly crushed.

The Argos

The Toronto Argonauts—originally a rugby team—is the oldest sports team in North America to keep its original name. The "Argos" started in 1873 as a branch of the Toronto Argonauts Rowing Club (which also still exists). Rugby in Canada gradually evolved, under American influence, into Canadian football. The Argonauts have won the Grey Cup, the Canadian Football League's premier award, 15 times.

Tiger-Cats

The Hamilton Tiger-Cats were formed in 1950, as a merger of the Hamilton Tigers and the Hamilton Flying Wildcats. They've won the Grey Cup eight times since joining together.

The Rough Riders and Renegades

The Ottawa Rough Riders date back to 1876 (though they only adopted their name in 1898, which caused much confusion with the Saskatchewan Roughriders, who spelled it as one word). The Rough Riders and the Roughriders played four Grey Cup finals against each other, with Ottawa winning three. The Rough Riders team folded in 1996. Between 2002 and 2006, the Ottawa Renegades played in the CFL. In 2006, they offered themselves for sale for $1 to anyone who would assume the team's massive debt. When no potential owner came forward, the league suspended the team.

Pa Bell

In 1874, Alexander Graham Bell ran experiments in his father's house in Brantford that would lead to the invention of the telephone. Canadians, Britons and Americans all claim Bell as their own. In fact, he was born in Scotland, and after spending a few years in Ontario and Québec, took a teaching job in Boston, got married and became an American citizen. He officially announced his invention of the telephone in the U.S. and patented it there first. Years later, though, he returned to Canada to retire in Cape Breton.

Telephones took off quickly in Ontario. In 1876, the world's first "long-distance" telephone call was made from Brantford to Paris (Paris, Ontario, that is!). The first telephone exchange in Canada opened in 1878 in Hamilton. By 1881, 400 Torontonians had telephones.

James Naismith of Almonte invented basketball in 1892. He had been teaching at a school in the United States and saw a need for an indoor sport that could be played in the winter. Under Naismith's original rules, peach baskets were used instead of nets, and players could only pass the ball, not dribble it.

His Home Was His Castle

Electricity tycoon Sir Henry Pellatt built Casa Loma in 1911 on Spadina Hill overlooking Toronto. (The name "Casa Loma" means "house on the hill" in Spanish; it was coined by a previous owner and was associated with the property before the construction of the famous Casa Loma.) The flamboyant mansion was designed to look like a full-sized medieval castle and set Sir Henry back some $3.5 million (in 1911 dollars). Some of its cooler features include a secret passage between Sir Henry's office and his wine cellar, an indoor pool (never completed) and an underground tunnel connecting the castle to its stables (also designed to look like a castle).

Bad business decisions soon bankrupted Sir Henry and he was forced to sell the house before it was completed. He died in 1939 with $185.08 in the bank and $6000 in debts. In 1937, Casa Loma became a city-owned museum, recreating the lavish lifestyle and décor of its heyday. Just before his death, Sir Henry himself visited the castle as an ordinary guest and signed the guestbook.

DID YOU KNOW?

On September 15, 1885, an unscheduled train in St. Thomas, hit Jumbo, the world's biggest elephant. His trainer was leading him across the tracks during the Barnum and Bailey Circus' stopover in the town. The collison derailed the train and the massive pachyderm was killed instantly. St. Thomas became well known because of the story, and in 1985, the town put up a full-sized statue of Jumbo to commemorate the 100th anniversary of his death.

Jumbo the elephant gave birth to the word "jumbo," meaning gigantic. Jumbo himself got the name at his original home in the London (UK) Zoo as a mispronunciation of *jambo*, the Swahili word for "hello."

The Great Fire of 1904

On April 19, 1904, most of downtown Toronto was destroyed by fire. The Great Fire itself lasted two days and caused $1 million damage (in 1904 dollars), put 5000 people out of work and wiped out many historic Georgian buildings. It smouldered for two weeks. Despite an investigation, no cause was ever determined for the fire. It remains a mystery.

Ontario Hydro: Smokin'

It was cigars that led to public electricity in Ontario. Sir Adam Beck, a German Canadian cigar manufacturer, complained that privately owned generators were gouging businesses on electricity. He became mayor of London and later a minister in Sir James P. Whitney's provincial government. In 1905, he convinced Whitney to nationalize electric power in Ontario, and Beck became the first head of the new utility, later known as Ontario Hydro.

Ontario's first big power plant—the hydro generator at Niagara Falls—was renamed the Sir Adam Beck Power Station after Beck died.

Five-Pin Bowling

Aside from the invention of basketball, one of Ontario's biggest (and smallest additions) to the world of games is five-pin bowling. It was invented in Toronto in 1909 as a way to increase bowling's popularity by allowing it to be played more quickly, during lunch breaks and before dinner.

Anne of Ontario

Despite her association with Prince Edward Island, Lucy Maude Montgomery actually lived nearly half her life in Ontario and wrote 17 out of her 20 novels there. She had three homes in the province—first in Uxbridge in 1911, then in Halton Hills and finally in Toronto, where she died in 1942. The popular television series *Road to Avonlea*, based on several of Montgomery's novels, was actually filmed in Uxbridge.

The Great War, the Great Thirst and the Great Depression: A Clash of Visions (1914–1939)

These years were tough for Ontario. Thousands of Ontarians never came back from the Great War. Those who did found jobs scarce and had to deal with the chaos of Prohibition, a law that forbade the sale of alcohol.

Prohibition pitted urban and rural Ontario against each other and launched a whole world of large-scale organized crime. From there, things got even worse, as the Depression shut down the industrial cities of the province and, as in Europe, caused many people to look to communism and fascism for answers.

THE GREAT WAR

Bishop and Brown

Billy Bishop burst out of Owen Sound to become Canada's
biggest hero of World War I and the Commonwealth's greatest
ace pilot. He was given the Victoria Cross for bringing down
three German planes in one outing, and in total, Bishop was
credited with 72 kills over the course of the war. Some historians have questioned Bishop's accomplishments—he had a reputation as a reckless self-promoter and was helped out by the
Canadian government, happy to use Bishop's name for propaganda purposes.

Another Ontario fighter pilot who made headlines was Roy
Brown of Carleton Place. He was best known for shooting down
and killing the great German ace Manfred von Richthofen, better known as the "Red Baron." Historians have since disputed
this claim and now tend to give credit to Australian ground
troops who had also been taking shots at von Richthofen when
his plane went down.

DID YOU KNOW?

John McCrea, a physician from Guelph, penned "In Flanders
Fields," the famous poem about World War I soldiers' final rest-
ing places. McCrea himself was killed in action soon afterwards.
The poem helped popularize the poppy as an international symbol of remembrance.

The Kaiser Takes a Tumble
In a fit of patriotic fervour during World War I, the town of
Berlin was renamed Kitchener, after the popular British Field
Marshal Horatio Kitchener. He was particularly famous for
appearing on "Kitchener Wants You!" propaganda posters

(which later inspired the American "Uncle Sam Wants You!" recruitment posters). Berlin, Ontario, was still mostly German-speaking during World War I and featured a bust of Kaiser Wilhelm II displayed in a park. The bust was torn down and thrown into a lake during the war and later disappeared. The German-Canadian Business and Professional Association, which had originally paid for the bust, had the pedestal on which it stood erected again in 1996, with a plaque about the "Kaiser's" disappearance.

During the war, many immigrants from enemy countries, including Germany and Austria, as well as parts of the Austro-Hungarian empire, such as the Ukraine and the Czech Republic, were put into forced labour camps in northern Ontario. During World War II, Japanese Ontarians got similar, but even more repressive, treatment.

On November 11, 1918—Armistice Day—Grunwald, a popular Muskoka resort with a German name, was burned down.

The "Jenny Canuck" was the first airplane ever built in Ontario, manufactured in 1915 by the Toronto branch of the American-based Curtiss Company. Incidentally, the word "Canuck" goes back to the early 19th century as an American slang word for "French Canadian." It was originally offensive, but later became an ordinary term for any Canadian. By the early 20th century, "Johnny Canuck" and "Jenny Canuck" were being used as nicknames for the average Canadian.

Saved by the Librarian
In 1916, Canada's beautiful first Parliament Buildings burned. Only the parliamentary library was saved, thanks to the librarian remembering to close its huge metal doors. The buildings were immediately rebuilt and reopened in 1920. The new design included the famous Peace Tower (replacing the Victoria Tower,

which had been built, ironically, in a German style), commemorating the end of World War I. Conspiracy theorists immediately blamed German agents for burning the building, but an investigation proved that it was something more banal—a lit cigar left in one of the lounges.

DID YOU  **KNOW?**

In 1917, Premier Howard Hearst allowed women to vote in provincial elections in Ontario—at least, non-aboriginal women over the age of 21. It may have been a miscalculation on Hearst's part, because he lost the next election in 1919. The female vote was credited with his defeat.

PROHIBITION

UFO Sighting

In 1918, a UFO appeared in Ontario—and it was soon getting
lots of votes. The United Farmers of Ontario (UFO) was a protest party that formed after World War I and caught everyone
by surprise—including its own supporters—by winning the
1919 election. At the time, it didn't even have a leader. The
UFO represented mainly rural voters, but it made alliances with
organized labour, which won it votes in urban areas. It wanted
Prohibition—which had started during the war—to continue.
This may have been a factor in the UFO's sudden disappearance
(possibly to another planet) after losing the 1923 election.

Banting is Best; Best is Left Out

In one of Canada's best-known medical breakthroughs, Dr.
Frederick Banting and his student, Charles Best, invented insu-
lin in a University of Toronto lab in 1921. The discovery won
Banting and the U of T Physiology Department head J.J.R.
MacLeod the Nobel Prize for Medicine in 1923. Controversially,
Best was not offered the prize—but Banting publicly shared his
award with the student.

Ontario Dries Up

Prohibition began in 1916 in Ontario and was upheld in a referendum in 1921. But the vote was narrow, and in every major
city, the majority voted against Prohibition.

Actually, some towns and rural areas already had Prohibition
before 1916, thanks to referendums in the late 19th century.
A local referendum in Toronto in 1877 voted against Prohibition.
It prompted days of rioting between "wets" and "dries" and a rau-
cous, drunken victory parade by the wets.

Oddly, according to the Prohibition Act of the day, it was only legal to manufacture alcohol, not sell it. At first—before the practice was outlawed—Ontario brewers and distillers simply exported their products to Québec, where alcohol sales were still legal. Thirsty Ontarians then ordered drinks (often made in Ontario) from Montréal by mail order. After laws were enacted against this, liquor manufacturers claimed that they had found a booming export market in Mexico and Cuba. In fact, most of their "exports" were being sold illegally in Ontario and in the United States, which had started its own Prohibition. In July 1920, an average of 1000 cases of whiskey were estimated to be illegally crossing the Windsor-Detroit border every day. During the 1920s, about 80 percent of Canadian beer and 60 percent of Canadian whiskey shipped to the United States is said to have passed across the St. Clair River.

Preacher Packing Heat

In 1921, a special squad of vigilantes, led by Reverend Les
Spracklin (who thought nothing of carrying a gun to uphold
morality) was appointed by the attorney general to prowl the
Windsor border. Spracklin was acquitted of manslaughter after
he shot dead a rum-runner (whose house he'd broken into), but
became unpopular and was forced to disband the squad. To
celebrate Spracklin's defeat, his opponents held the wildly
debauched (and daringly openly advertised) Bootleggers Ball.

Rocco Perri

Ontario's "King of the Bootleggers," and the province's first millionaire criminal, was Italian immigrant Rocco Perri. Posing as
a simple macaroni salesman, Perri and his wife Bessie Starkman
owned an enormous house in Hamilton and several expensive
cars. In a sensational interview with the *Toronto Star* in 1924,
Perri admitted to being a bootlegger, but defended the trade.
Rival American gangsters eventually murdered Starkman and
tried to kill Perri by bombing his car. In 1944, he simply disappeared without a trace.

Booze as Big Business

Perri became a millionaire on profits from bootlegging in
Ontario, but the real money was in the exportation of alcohol
to the United States, and these operations were usually directed
from even more opulent mansions in Montréal. The Bronfman
family first grew rich shipping alcohol across the border through
the Prairies. Sir Mortimer Davis profited mainly from smuggling through Ontario.

Davis, the aristocratic owner of Imperial Tobacco and the
Canadian Industrial Alcohol Company, was too respected to
involve himself directly in smuggling, but he hired two Ontario
brothers, Herb and Harry Hatch, to do his dirty work.

Hatching a Plan

The Hatch brothers, former bartenders, were both experienced smugglers. They assembled a fleet of fishing boats in eastern Lake Ontario (and an army of indentured fishermen) by buying up control of mortgages on the vessels. The flothilla soon became known as "Hatch's Navy." The Hatches later ditched Sir Mortimer to set out on their own, buying the massive abandoned Gooderham & Worts distillery in Toronto from its owners, the brothers William and Sir Robert Gooderham. Eventually, as American coast guard boats became more sophisticated, the Hatches were the only ones capable of outrunning them, and they gained a near monopoly on rum-running in Ontario. They went on to buy the Hiram Walker distillery in Windsor and became the biggest alcohol producers and sellers in Canada. After Prohibition ended, the Hatch brothers, always keeping a low profile, blended into Toronto's high society. (Harry later became well known as a racehorse owner; his horses won the Queen's Plate five times.)

Stranger than a Three-Dollar Bill

Prohibition produced plenty of eccentric characters, such as "Dollar" Bill Allen, a small-time Kingston rum-runner who ran his business from an abandoned aircraft hanger (where he also lived and was known to drink and play poker with local judges). He was notorious for handing out money and sodas to poor children, playing hockey with them and cycling around town in ridiculous getups, chased by urchins. Police usually left him alone because of his charity and because the profits he made from alcohol were so low (unlike most other bootleggers, Allen sold drinks at low prices). He was arrested one time and fined $100—but only after defending himself and telling the court his life story several times. He spoke so fast and used such flowery language that the court stenographer was unable to keep up.

King Cole was a Rum-Running Soul

Another creation of Prohibition was Claude "King" Cole, the owner of Main Duck Island, near Belleville. As his nickname suggests, Cole ran the island as his own private kingdom, complete with a colony of fishermen who operated his smuggling boats and a lighthouse that could be conveniently turned off and on at his choosing. He populated the island with racehorses and wild Plains buffalo that he bought from the Hamilton Zoo.

Strongman, Weak Beer

Premier G. Howard Ferguson was known for his autocratic style, once telling his successor, George Henry, that "the average fellow likes to be dictated to and controlled." Ferguson also promoted a light beer—nicknamed "Fergy's Foam"—as a compromise between Prohibition's supporters and opponents. The beer had a 4.4 percent alcohol content, above the 2.5 percent limit imposed by Prohibition, but below the stiff 9 percent beer that had been the standard before. The *Toronto Star* offered a $100 prize to the first person to get drunk on the watery beer, but the prize was never claimed.

Fergy's Foam did not go over well, and in 1927, after dozens of Ontarians had died from drinking poisonous moonshine, Ferguson's government finally killed Prohibition. Unfortunately for Ontario drinkers, Ferguson replaced it with the Liquor Control Board of Ontario and some of the most restrictive alcohol regulations in Canada.

THE TIMES CHANGE

Standard Time

In 1929, standard time and its system of time zones were adopted around the world. Sir Sandford Fleming, a railway surveyor, had proposed the idea of standard time to the Royal Canadian Institute, a national scientific society, back in 1879. He continued to promote it internationally. Sir Sandford Fleming College in Lindsay was later named after him.

Ambrose Small

In one of Ontario's most sensational mysteries, theatre tycoon Ambrose Small disappeared on December 1, 1919. Just before he vanished, he inexplicably sold all of his theatre empire for $1.7 million—but he didn't take the money with him. Police found no reliable leads to explain his disappearance and finally closed the case, still unsolved, in 1960.

Agnes MacPhail

Agnes MacPhail made history as the first women elected to federal Parliament in 1921. She was also one of the first two women elected to provincial parliament in 1943.

First Load

In 1927, the first washing machine capable of agitating clothes was invented in Fergus by the Beatty Brothers Company. One year later, Maytag came out with its own agitating washer and dominated the industry.

Stealing the Tracks

During the 1920s, copper prices rose so high that in 1929 it was reported that thieves were actually chipping at the copper bonds of the streetcar tracks in Toronto.

Ku Klux Klan

The Ku Klux Klan entered Ontario in the 1920s but never gained much popularity compared to other provinces (especially Saskatchewan where it became temporarily influential). Still, it was praised in many major newspapers—including the Toronto *Globe* and *Star*—for its anti-black activities.

Ferguson versus Ford

Although auto manufacturing was Ontario's biggest industry, Premier Ferguson was not shy about expressing his dislike of cars. He never owned one and once told a group of his supporters that the car was a curse on human civilization. The next day, the Ford Motor Company's lawyers threatened to sue him.

Royal York Hotel

On June 11, 1929, just months before the onset of the Great Depression, the Royal York Hotel opened its doors in Toronto. It was an impressive structure and the flagship of the Canadian Pacific hotel chain. At the time, it was not only the tallest building in Toronto, but also the tallest in the Commonwealth. It kept both titles for only a year, though, before being beaten out by the Canadian Bank of Commerce tower a few blocks away.

THE GREAT DEPRESSION

Children of the Depression

On May 28, 1934, the Dionne quintuplets were born between the towns of Corbeil and Callander (near North Bay). The provincial government took the five girls away from their impoverished parents and converted them into the country's biggest tourist attraction of the decade (at one point, more people were coming to see the "quints" in Quintland, their zoo-like compound, than were going to see Niagara Falls). In Quintland, gawking tourists could pay to view the children through two-way mirrors; it was even suggested that they be moved into the abandoned Casa Loma in Toronto to score even bigger profits. They were the first known case of quintuplets surviving childbirth, but the events of their childhood scarred Yvonne, Annette, Cécile, Émilie and Marie for life. In 1998, the three surviving Quints successfully sued the Ontario government to recoup some of the profits it had made from them.

DID YOU KNOW?

Although not as hard hit as the Prairies, Ontario suffered badly during the Great Depression. Unemployment was high, and people became restless. Town councillors and mayors were often at the frontlines of fights. In 1936, citizens of Stamford Township, now part of Niagara Falls, locked up eight municipal officials in the town hall, demanding higher welfare payments. The Etobicoke reeve was also imprisoned similarly. The mayor of Fort Erie shot back that all men on welfare should be sterilized.

Glenn Gould

Glenn Gould was born in Toronto in 1932 (his last name was originally Gold, but the family changed it to avoid anti-Semitism, even though they were not Jewish). Gould went on to become Canada's best-known classical pianist—and also its most eccentric. While performing (he specialized in Bach), Gould refused to play unless he sat on a folding chair, made by his father, which was forever falling apart. He refused to be touched and often wore heavy work clothes instead of the standard tuxedo. He also would eat nothing but scrambled eggs (prepared in a particular way) for long periods.

Christie Pits Riot

Christie Pits Park, a former gravel pit that was named after the nearby Christie Biscuit Factory (of "Mr. Christie, you make good cookies" fame) was the site of Toronto's worst race riot. The Christie Pits riot of 1933 started when an Anglo baseball team, playing in the park's diamond, started taunting the opposing, partly Jewish team with a swastika banner and shouts of "Heil Hitler." The fight—which lasted all day and ended with the swastika being ripped up—saw around 10,000 youths arrive by the truckload with chains and bats. Police seemed to show little interest in intervening.

The poverty of the Depression, and the apparent success of
Hitler in Germany, had turned some English Torontonians
towards fascism. The "swastika clubs" of young men tried to
start other fights, including attempts to force Jews off the public
beaches (they put up signs saying "No Jews or Dogs" and physi-
cally assaulted a number of beach-goers).

Fascism

Meeting at Toronto's Massey Hall in 1938, Canadian fascists
tried to organize something called the "National Unity Party"
out of their various groups (with the assistance of the German
and Italian consulates). Eighty-five uniformed members stood in
formation to inspect the members of the public coming to the
meeting. Local Nazi leader, Joseph Farr, and Québec fascist,
Adrien Arcand, both harangued the crowd with anti-Semitic
speeches. The police, for their part, offered the fascists protec-
tion and used their mounted units to beat and scatter protestors
who had gathered across the street. Hitler's aggression in Europe
and the beginning of World War II quickly brought an end to
fascism's growing popularity in Ontario, though racism and
anti-Semitism continued to linger in some areas.

King's Follies

Kitchener's William Lyon Mackenzie King, grandson of the
1837 rebel William Lyon Mackenzie, was an odd character, to
say the least. After his death, it became known that he regularly
attended séances and claimed to converse with the spirits of his
dead mother and his dog (as well as such well-known luminaries
as Leonardo da Vinci). After his party lost a by-election in
1938, King expressed shock in his diary, saying: "I have never
been deceived by a vision," adding that it just might be a good
idea to place less trust in "visions, dreams and impressions." In
fact, he had been deceived before. In 1934, the ghost of Sir
Wilfrid Laurier apparently told King that his hated fellow

Liberal, Mitch Hepburn would lose the Ontario provincial election—something that did not come to pass.

King was also naïve enough to believe that Hitler could be placated, and he supported British Prime Minister Neville Chamberlain's attempts to appease the German leader. In fact, King credited himself with introducing Chamberlain to Hitler's ambassador, leading to the unsuccessful peace pact with Germany.

King was a critic of the British aristocracy and an advocate of total Canadian independence from Britain. Nevertheless, he was so impressed by King George VI and Queen Elizabeth that he told them he was prepared to lay his life at their feet "in helping to further great causes which they have at heart."

George McCullagh and the Leadership League

George McCullagh, the self-made businessman and so-called "Boy Millionaire" who had merged the *Globe* with the *Mail and Empire* in 1936, soon began to advocate a kind of fascism himself. He blamed indecision and bureaucracy for the Depression, and promoted decisive single-party, single-tier government (this included merging the federal Conservative and Liberal parties and doing away with provinces altogether). McCullagh shamelessly publicized his group—called the "Leadership League"—through the *Globe and Mail.* In 1939, he claimed 125,000 members, including Sir Frederick Banting, co-inventor of insulin, and Dr. Herbert Bruce, the former lieutenant-governor. But almost as quickly as it sprang up, the Leadership League's support disappeared, and McCullagh was forced to shut it down. The same year, McCullagh's horse won the King's Plate, and King George VI handed him the prize (Prime Minister King, who hated McCullagh, suspected that he had fixed the race to get an audience with George VI and restart his career in politics). In fact, McCullagh never again returned to politics, and after suffering from manic depression for years, killed himself in 1952. He was the model for the character Percy "Boy" Staunton in Robertson Davies' popular novel *Fifth Business.*

Red Scare

Police and governments treated communists and suspected communists harshly. In 1933, Ontario Provincial Police motorcycle constables shut down a meeting of suspected communists in Toronto's High Park by encircling it and running their engines with the exhaust pipes pointed inwards.

The Communist Party, for some time using the pseudonym "Labour Progressive Party," reached its height on Ontario in the 1930s, but never posed much of a threat to the government. Nevertheless, it was considered a major problem by the authorities and was regularly attacked. Prime Minister R.B. Bennett offered to crush them under the "iron heel of ruthlessness."

Toronto Mayor Sam McBride (after whom one of the Toronto Island ferries is now named) said "our stopping of Communist meetings shows that we are truly British." Despite the criticisms of communists as anti-British, almost all Communist Party leaders were recent British immigrants. York County deputy reeve, Harry Meighan, claimed that 1000 armed communists were training for a raid of the Eaton's and Simpson's grocery departments. Most of the Communist Party's leadership, based in Toronto, was arrested and put in Kingston Penitentiary (leader Tim Buck was denied access to Hansard, the parliamentary record, while in jail, because there were "too many radical specches in it"). He was later almost assassinated, as guards fired a number of shots, from a distance, into his cell.

How About a Public-Private Partnership?
In 1931, chief justice of Ontario, Sir William Mulock, claimed that communists planned to "nationalize women."

Stratford before Shakespeare
Today, most people think of Stratford, Ontario, as a picturesque tourist town famous for its Shakespearean theatre and the beautiful Avon River. (In fact, the Avon is really a narrow creek—it

was only recently dammed at each end of downtown to simulate
the width of the original Avon River in Stratford, UK.)

During the 1920s and 1930s, Stratford was a heavily industrial-
ized railway and manufacturing town. It won the nickname
"Communist Capital of Canada" because of the militancy of the
railway workers' unions. Local politicians were quick to capital-
ize. The mayor supposedly cut his moustache to look like Stalin.
In 1933, the provincial government, with the help of the army,
including tank and artillery units, put down a bitter strike in
Stratford.

Spanish Civil War

About 1400 Canadians, mostly entering through the recruitment
office at the corners of Queen and Spadina Streets in Toronto,
signed up to fight in the Spanish Civil War. Half of them never
returned. Known as the Mackenzie-Papineau Battalion (after the
leaders of the 1837 Rebellions), the volunteers fought to support
the Spanish government against the Nazi Germany–backed
General Francisco Franco. After Franco's victory and Stalin's
refusal to send Russian troops to support them, the survivors
limped back to Canada, in some cases unable to pay their fares.
A small marching band greeted their return to Toronto, but
mostly they were ignored. Later, when World War II started,
many of the Spanish Civil War veterans were among the first to
sign up to fight again (though some of them, suspected communists, were turned down).

The biggest name to come out of Ontario's contribution to the
Spanish Civil War was Gravenhurst's Dr. Norman Bethune.
While travelling with the Mackenzie-Papineau Battalion,
Bethune developed the modern military medical unit system.
He later died while working in China and was eulogized in
a pamphlet by Mao Tsetung, which made him world famous
(and the namesake of a number of hospitals, schools and
streets in Canada and China).

Hepburn's Hussars

When workers went on strike at the Oshawa General Motors plant in 1937, Premier Mitchell Hepburn tried to get the RCMP to shut down the protest. But Prime Minister King refused to send the Mounties in, so Hepburn organized a mounted volunteer force—sarcastically nicknamed "Hepburn's Hussars" or the "Sons of Mitches"—with which he threatened to force the strikers back to work. Within weeks, Hepburn relented and gave in to the union.

Despite his fearsome attacks on unions and suspected communists, Hepburn went on to make a formal alliance with the Communist Party (known as the "Labour Progressive Party" at the time) and actually ran several candidates with them in 1945.

Provincial Car Sale
One of Hepburn's first acts on coming into office in 1934 was to sell off the fleet of luxury cars used by the premier and cabinet ministers of the previous Conservative government. Hepburn—ever a showman—had the cars auctioned off in front of a roaring crowd in Toronto's Varsity Stadium.

He also shut down Chorley Park, the official residence of the lieutenant-governor and Toronto's most opulent home, located in the elite Rosedale neighbourhood. Sadly, Chorley Park, built in 1912 in the style of a French castle, was later torn down.

Not Leader… Still Leader

In 1942, Premier Hepburn resigned his position after a fight with Prime Minister King. Hepburn appointed Gordon Daniel Conant as the new premier but kept the position of head of the Liberal Party for himself—something almost unprecedented. Angry members of Parliament forced him to resign that, too, but in 1944, they asked him to return, and Hepburn became leader again that year.

Big Blue Machine

Ontario gained a reputation as a Conservative province after the "Big Blue Machine" of the Progressive Conservative Party took power in 1943 and held it until 1985.

A Province Fit for a King

In 1939, King George VI and Queen Elizabeth (who later became the Queen Mother) visited Canada. Despite centuries of British involvement on the continent, they were the first British monarchs to visit North America. The couple escaped their handlers and waded into a crowd of supporters in Ottawa. It amazed the public, and the press immediately contrasted the informality of the royals with the rigid, distant public personas of Hitler and Stalin. It was the first "walkabout"—now a tradition (albeit a carefully controlled one) for royals.

In Recent News: Hippies and Leafs (1939 Onwards)

World War II put a clear end to the Depression in Ontario and launched the province into a new world— one populated by Cold War paranoia, strange, long-haired people and more...

WORLD WAR II

DID YOU  KNOW?

One of the world's most covert military training camps operated in a location between Whitby and Oshawa in 1941. "Camp X," as it was known, secretly trained Canadians and Britons—and even more surreptitiously, Americans, before that country's official entry into World War II—in espionage techniques. Sir Ian Fleming, the British secret agent who later wrote the James Bond novels, partly based on his own experiences in espionage, got his start at Camp X, as did many CIA agents.

100,000 Tulips

Princess Juliana of the Netherlands (who later became its queen) gave birth to a daughter, Princess Margaret, in Ottawa Civic Hospital in 1945. Because of the Nazi occupation of the Netherlands, the royal family had escaped to seek refuge in Canada. The government declared the hospital ward to be, temporarily, part of the Netherlands, so it could be said that Margaret was born on Dutch soil. Because of this—and because Canadian soldiers liberated the Netherlands—the two countries have had a close relationship. In 1945, Juliana donated 100,000 tulip bulbs to be planted in Ottawa and 20,000 have been sent every year since.

DID YOU  KNOW?

German Luftwaffe officer, Franz von Werra, was the only one out of 30,000 Axis POWs to successfully escape from a Canadian prison camp. In 1941, he jumped off a train carrying German prisoners near Smiths Falls and walked through the woods to Prescott, where he stole a rowboat and used it to cross the St. Lawrence River. At the time, the U.S. was still neutral, and he was able to openly approach the German consulate in New York City. The consulate secretly transported him to Mexico and then back to Germany. Von Werra's daring escape featured prominently in German propaganda, but he died shortly after returning to duty, when his plane disappeared over the English Channel.

GROWTH, THE COLD WAR, HIPPIES AND CIVIL RIGHTS

The Boyd Gang

Dapper ex-soldier Edwin Alonzo Boyd and his "Boyd Gang" turned Toronto upside down with a series of daring bank robberies in the late 1940s and early 1950s. In 1952, two Boyd Gang members were hanged for their roles in a murder, but Boyd himself only spent 14 years behind bars before being paroled. He died in British Columbia in 2002. After his death, tapes surfaced in which he confessed to "dispatching" a young couple in Toronto in 1947 as "practice," after he ran into them by coincidence one night. The murders had been unsolved up to that time. He posed brandishing a pistol just before his death.

Bell Lap

In 1954, Marilyn Bell of Toronto was the first person to swim across Lake Ontario. She completed the 52-kilometre distance from Toronto to Rochester, New York, in 21 hours.

Hurricane Hazel

The worst storm ever to hit Ontario was Hurricane Hazel in 1954—one of very few hurricanes to make it so far inland. Nearly 100 people were killed, primarily in Toronto and in rural areas north of the city. Toronto's Humber River rose so high that low-lying houses along its shores were washed away. The water pressure also broke the dikes that protected the Holland Marsh, built below sea level, and submerged the whole area.

Toronto opened its subway system—the first in Canada—in 1954. It was free to ride on the first day (but the price hasn't stopped going up since!). The subway was originally a single line, going up Yonge Street from Union Station to Eglinton Avenue. The second line, along Bloor and Danforth Streets, was opened in 1966, the same year that Montréal launched its underground Métro system. Toronto's system remains the largest—though its austere, narrow stations stand in contrast to the much more elaborate ones in Montréal. Toronto's subway is much nearer to the surface than most others, and its tracks closely follow major streets. This was because the original lines were built by digging trenches down the middle of streets, into which the tracks were lowered. Afterwards, when the tunnels were finished, they were covered over. Most subway systems are built by the more expensive process of tunnelling, rather than trenching.

The Lost Villages

The St. Lawrence Seaway was opened in 1959 to let larger ships pass through the St. Lawrence River, but the flooding necessary to expand the river destroyed several towns in eastern Ontario. The towns of Milles Roches, Moulinette, Wales, Dickenson's Landing, Farran's Point, Aultsville and the smaller hamlets of Maple Grove, Santa Cruz, Woodlands and Sheik's Islands were deliberately submerged. Today, the Lost Villages Museum in Long Sault recalls the sunken towns and displays artifacts from them.

Civil Rights

Most Canadians think of the southern U.S. in the 1960s when they think of the Civil Rights Movement, but there was also an Ontario Civil Rights Movement. Many towns had passed discriminatory bylaws (Grand Bend apparently banned Jews and "Negroes" from owning property in 1948). In 1947, Hugh Burnett, a black Canadian war veteran, returned to his hometown of Dresden, Ontario. When a local restaurant, Kay's Café, refused to serve him because of his race, he started the National Unity Association (NUA) to fight discrimination. The NUA was able to get the Dresden Town Council to initiate a referendum on equality, but citizens voted it down. In fact, it seemed that other businesses were just as eager to keep blacks out. By the 1950s, Premier Leslie Frost's government passed anti-discrimination laws. In 1961, the Ontario Human Rights Code was passed.

Several black activists decided to test things by going back to Kay's Café in 1954, and after they were refused service again, started a lawsuit. In 1956, businesses in Dresden finally had to back down and allow blacks in, but the town took its revenge on Burnett by boycotting his carpentry businesses and forcing him to move.

DID YOU KNOW?

Ducking and covering was all right for the masses, but Cold War Canadian politicians had their own way of surviving a nuclear war—the "Diefenbunker." The massive underground network of offices and living quarters was built by Prime Minister John Diefenbaker in the town of Carp, near Ottawa (the name "Diefenbunker" was coined by Opposition politicians). It was one of a number of similar bunkers built across the country. In the event of a nuclear attack, federal politicians and military leaders were supposed to withdraw to the bomb-proof, radiation-proof shelter, which featured an emergency CBC broadcast centre and an austere prime ministerial suite. Today, the structure is open to the public as the Diefenbunker: Canada's Cold War Museum.

Prime Minister Diefenbaker cancelled construction of the Avro Arrow interceptor jet in 1959—putting thousands of employees at the Malton plant out of work—and quickly making him an unpopular figure in Ontario. (Diefenbaker was often portrayed as a westerner who knew little about Ontario issues, though he was actually born in Neustadt, north of Stratford.)

Diefenbaker had been pressured by the American government to scrap the project, which was producing the most advanced aircraft in the world at a lower cost than competing U.S. designs. After the cancellation, the Arrow prototypes were destroyed and dumped into Lake Ontario. Attempts to recover them have been unsuccessful.

Trudeaumania

In contrast to Québec and the West, where late Prime Minister Pierre Trudeau remains mostly unpopular, he is fondly remembered in Ontario. It was frequently said, up until the time of his death in 2000, that Trudeau could have won any seat in Ontario by a landslide, even if he didn't campaign. While in office, Trudeau received the bulk of his support in Ontario, and he was particularly well liked for his pro-immigration policies. Many first and second generation immigrants in Ontario continue to revere Trudeau. A statue of him was built in the mostly Italian Toronto suburb of Woodbridge after his death.

Yorkville: the Northern Haight

It's hard to believe that Toronto's ritziest neighbourhood was once a hippie hub. As flower power culture spread across North America in the 1960s, the poor, mostly immigrant neighbourhood of Yorkville was taken over by hairy, hygienically deficient young people. It soon became a local tourist magnet, as people came to take in folk music in the coffeehouses and gawk at the strange-looking people sprawled around, not unlike San Francisco's famous Haight-Ashbury district.

The hippie colony quickly became a victim of its own success as a spectacle: once enough wealthy tourists were drawn to the area, local business owners no longer had a need for the long-haired types. The police had them pushed out, sometimes violently. Reaction towards hippies from Toronto's Establishment was harsh. Former Toronto Maple Leafs captain, Syl Apps, who chaired Parliament's Select Committee on Youth, called Yorkville a "festering sore on the face of the city" in 1967. A mostly unsubstantiated panic started when it was reported that a number of hippies had hepatitis C from sharing needles. City officials told the public to stay away from Yorkville, and bemused (and upset) flower children often found crowds of people—who believed that the hippies had the disease and that it was airborne—running away from them. By the end of the 1960s, counter-culture Yorkville had been shut down. The working-class families of the previous generation were forced to leave as well, because rents skyrocketed and the area was overtaken by boutiques and offices.

Rochdale College

Only a few blocks down Bloor Street from Yorkville was Rochdale College, the wild experiment in alternative education that ran from 1968 to 1975. The 18-storey free university started with a group of idealistic professors and students, but was eventually shut down because of its disorganization and central role in the city's drug scene. Rochdale's use of Hells Angels as security guards didn't help its reputation. (The hippies in the College were friendlier than the Angels, sometimes greeting police raids with balloons and confetti and even a cake reading "Welcome 52 Division.")

CANADA'S FAVOURITE SPORT

The Good Old Hockey Game

Ontario boasts the most commercially successful hockey team in the National Hockey League (NHL)—even if they haven't won the Stanley Cup since 1967.

The Maple Leafs team has won the Stanley Cup 13 times since 1918 (though they won their first two cups under different team names—as the Arenas and the St. Patricks). Their last win in 1967 was a surprise victory over their highly favoured arch-rival, the Montréal Canadiens.

After that, the Leafs went into long-term decline, hitting rock bottom in the 1980s under infamous owner Harold Ballard. Until his death in 1990, Ballard was probably the least popular man in Toronto. He was known for his perpetually irate disposition and his refusal to spend money to sign skilled players— though he did everything he could to squeeze more seats into Maple Leaf Gardens, including taking down the Queen's picture to free up more room.

Maple Leaf Gardens, built in 1931, was the last of the original six NHL hockey arenas to survive. The Leafs left it for the new Air Canada Centre in 1999. They've shared the building with the Raptors, Toronto's National Basketball Association team since 1995. (Before this, the last pro basketball team to play in the city was the Toronto Huskies, between 1946 and 1947.)

It looks almost certain that Maple Leaf Gardens will be turned into a Loblaws supermarket, despite considerable public outcry against it. "Our bakery manager may get called for icing," says an advertisement on the side of the building.

The famous hockey phrase "He shoots, he scores!" was coined by commentator Foster Hewitt at the Gardens. Hewitt—who provided commentary for hockey games from 1923 to 1972—was also known for his gondola, a unique contraption that give him a bird's-eye view of the Gardens' ice.

DID YOU  KNOW?

Three of Canada's best known folk singers of the 1960s and 1970s—Stompin' Tom Connors, Stan Rogers and Gordon Lightfoot—all have close connections to Ontario. Despite his western cowboy image, Connors was born in New Brunswick, and in 1964, got his start in music in Timmins, where he was working as a miner. Many of Stan Rogers' fans would be surprised to hear that he was born and raised in Hamilton. His parents were from Nova Scotia and Rogers was strongly connected to the revival of Nova Scotian folksongs. He died in a plane accident in 1977. Gordon Lightfoot was born in Orillia in 1938 and gained superstardom in the 1970s with songs such as, "The Wreck of the Edmund Fitzgerald."

Senators

The Ottawa Senators, founded in 1901, are actually older than the Maple Leafs—though they didn't exist between 1934 and 1992. Frank Finnigan, the only surviving member of the original Ottawa Senators, helped promote its relaunch.

Toronto Grows

Toronto grew quickly after World War II. In the 1970s, thanks mainly to immigration, Toronto surpassed its old rival, Montréal, as Canada's largest city. Political instability in Québec caused many of the country's biggest companies to move their headquarters from Montréal to Toronto. At present—depending on how many of its suburbs you include—the Toronto area makes up between half and two-thirds of Ontario's population.

OTHER SPORTS AND CULTURE

Olympics

Toronto has bid unsuccessfully for the Summer Olympics several times. So far, the only Olympic event to be held in Ontario was the yacht race in the 1976 Montréal Olympics. It happened in Lake Ontario, at Kingston's Portsmouth Harbour (renamed Portsmouth Olympic Harbour), because there was no suitable place in the Montréal area.

CN Tower

The CN Tower was completed in 1976, after three years of construction. It (deliberately) nosed just slightly taller than Moscow's Ostankino Tower to become the world's tallest free-standing building. As of the print date of this book, it still holds that title—but three new buildings, in Australia, the United Arab Emirates and Chicago, are set to surpass it.

Blue Jays

The Toronto Blue Jays played their first game in 1977. They were the second Canadian team to play Major League Baseball (after the now-defunct Montréal Expos). The team originally played in Exhibition Stadium—an unpopular building known as the "mistake by the lake." In 1989, the Jays moved to the SkyDome, where they went on to win the 1992 and 1993 World Series. The team has declined in popularity since then.

Another Attempt by the Lake

Soccer, also known as football, is—arguably—surpassing hockey to become the top spectator sport in Toronto. Traffic-jamming World Cup street parties through Little Portugal, Little Italy and Koreatown in 2006 seem to confirm this. Accordingly, a professional-scale football stadium is being built on the site of the old Exhibition Stadium, to house Toronto FC (Football Club), the city's newest pro sports team.

Tie-Dyed Magician

Canada's most famous magician, Doug Henning, was born in Winnipeg, but moved to Toronto at a young age. As a teenager, he had a magic show on a local TV station. He studied psychology at McMaster University in Hamilton. According to a McMaster legend, one of Henning's tricks was to make himself appear in the women's dorm.

He eventually made it onto mainstream American television in 1974 with *Doug Henning's World of Magic*, and was nominated for seven Emmy awards. Henning was most famous for his flamboyant stage persona—which involved tie-dyed clothes, long hair and a bushy moustache—and his general sense of humour.

Before his death in 2000, he had become a candidate for the Natural Law Party and often appeared on its commercials. Henning claimed that yogic meditation allowed him to fly. He also tried, unsuccessfully, to build a Natural Law Party theme park, called "Maharishi Veda Land," near Niagara Falls.

ABOUT THE AUTHOR
& ILLUSTRATORS

René Josef Biberstein

René Biberstein was born in Toronto and spent part of his childhood in Switzerland. He studied journalism at Concordia University, won the Concordia Media Award and was voted the best journalist on campus by his fellow students. He went on to freelance for Toronto's *Now* magazine, the *Montreal Mirror, Tart* and the *Globe and Mail Online Edition*. René also spent two years as a walking tour guide in southern Ontario. He is fascinated by the way places affect people's lives and plans to study urban planning at Ryerson University.

Roly Woods

Roly grew up in Indian River, Ontario. He has worked in Toronto as a freelance illustrator, and was also employed in the graphic design department of a landscape architecture firm specializing in themed retail and entertainment design. In 2004, he wrote and illustrated a historical comic book set in Lang Pioneer Village near Peterborough. Roly currently lives and works as a freelance illustrator in Calgary, Alberta, with his wife, Kerri, and their dog, Hank.

Roger Garcia

Roger Garcia immigrated to Canada from El Salvador at the age of seven. Because of the language barrier, he had to find a way to communicate with other kids. That's when he discovered the art of tracing. It wasn't long before he mastered this highly skilled technique, and by age 14, he was drawing weekly cartoons for the *Edmonton Examiner*. He also taught himself to paint and sculpt. Currently, Roger's work can be seen in a local weekly newspaper and in places around Edmonton.